T0354913

TRUSTING
IN
GOD'S
PLAN

TRUSTING IN GOD'S PLAN

Dealing With Cancer and
Disabilities By Way of Faith

AL LEAL

TRUSTING IN GOD'S PLAN
DEALING WITH CANCER AND
DISABILITIES BY WAY OF FAITH

iUniverse books may be ordered through booksellers or by contacting:

iUniverse
1663 Liberty Drive
Bloomington, IN 47403
www.iuniverse.com
844-349-9409

Because of the dynamic nature of the Internet, any web addresses or links contained in this book may have changed since publication and may no longer be valid. The views expressed in this work are solely those of the author and do not necessarily reflect the views of the publisher, and the publisher hereby disclaims any responsibility for them.

Any people depicted in stock imagery provided by Getty Images are models, and such images are being used for illustrative purposes only. Certain stock imagery © Getty Images.

ISBN: 978-1-6632-6449-7 (sc)
ISBN: 978-1-6632-6448-0 (e)

Library of Congress Control Number: 2024913651

Print information available on the last page.

iUniverse rev. date: 08/20/2024

All the stories in Trusting in God's Plan are true, depicting real people and their loved ones' journeys battling cancer and disabilities. The names of several of the interviewees and other persons mentioned herein have been changed to protect their identity.

CONTENTS

"Blessed is the man who trusts in the Lord,
and whose hope is the Lord."

—Jeremiah 17:7

To my two sons, Aurelio Matthew Leal and Daniel Alejandro Leal, who are the light of my life. They are my drive and my inspiration for continuing on my life's journey.

And especially to my late father, Aurelio Leal Sr., who provided the financial and moral support for the publication of this book.

PREFACE

Life is full of surprises that directly impact us either positively or negatively. These surprises can be detrimental to our health and well-being. At times, we perceive the worst or expect the worst. We tend to be lacking in belief and faith in God and His Son, our Lord and Savior, Jesus Christ.

We need to change our thoughts to make them more affirmative way and also embrace our faith. A close friend once told me, "I prefer to use three letters in my daily life: PMA."

I asked him, "What does that signify?"

He replied, "A positive mental attitude!" Then he repeated himself: "A positive mental attitude!"

You must leave your negative thoughts behind. Remember, positive thoughts yield positive results.

A famous author, Norman Vincent Peale, wrote important books on positive principles for living. I own a couple of them, but one in particular is of immense importance to me and stands out above the rest. It is an international bestseller, *The Power of Positive Thinking*—a great asset as it has influenced my mental attitude and behavior and has helped me to deal with life's struggles and, most recently, my battle with appendiceal cancer and COVID-19.

Never in my wildest dreams did I ever think I would come face-to-face with one of humanity's predominant and deadliest diseases, cancer, a disease that wreaks havoc on a person's life and the lives of his or her loved ones. This catastrophic disease results in hundreds of thousands of deaths in the United States and around the world each year. It does not discriminate, and it takes no prisoners. In the worst-case scenario, it has a devastating effect on innocent lives and affects many families, which are torn to shreds.

But how do we deal with cancer?

We cannot deny its existence and try to avoid it or even outwit it. It is deadly and has ruined many lives.

So, what do we do? How do we combat it?

We should continue to raise awareness and support our scientists in their quest to find a cure. Also, we must educate ourselves on the delicate subject of cancer.

To be more clear-cut, we can deal with cancer and any other health problem by accepting it, staying strong, having faith in God, and most importantly trusting in Him.

My experience with battling cancer has caused me to become a stronger person with a positive mental attitude and an immense love for and trust in God.

It is my hope that *Trusting in God's Plan* will be of use to the family members, loved ones, and friends of anyone who is currently battling or has previously battled cancer or other diseases or disabilities such as Down syndrome, autism, blindness, and cerebral palsy. These brave souls who must increase their hope through faith and place their entire lives in God's hands, trusting Him.

The stories I share herein are true. They illuminate the everyday struggles that people with certain diseases or disabilities, and their loved ones, face in seeking to live normal and successful lives. The individuals whose stories appear in *Trusting in God's Plan* are of true heroes who face their real-life challenges head-on, either alone or with the help of family members and friends.

Furthermore, *Trusting in God's Plan* provides insight into the lives of several different people and their unique journeys as they strive to live lives filled with faith, hope, and love. These people have embraced God's plan and believe in His good grace. Their unique faith and immense trust in God assists them in dealing with heart-wrenching obstacles and personal tragedies.

Their stories will make you understand that none of us is alone. God is by our sides.

During the process of publishing *Trusting in God's Plan*, my wife was diagnosed with breast cancer. She is now undergoing chemotherapy and is scheduled for surgery. And a friend of mine who is mentioned in one of the chapters herein was diagnosed with pancreatic cancer. He underwent several life-threatening surgeries and endured a lengthy stay at a Houston hospital. Unfortunately, the surgeons there brought him shocking news: there was nothing more they could do for him. He is currently at home in hospice care.

CHAPTER 1

―᠁ ✂ ᠁―

TRUST IN GOD

*Trust in the Lord with all thine heart; and lean not
unto thine own understanding.*

—Proverbs 3:5

In February 2018, my family and I relocated to San Antonio,
Texas, under the auspices of the US government, to which I had
dedicated myself in nearly twenty-nine years of loyal service.
I was now on the verge of retirement. I had plans to extend
my government service for another year. But I was not aware
of God's plan or what He had in store for me. A dramatic and
unfortunate event occurred and changed my life forever.

In May 2019, I experienced intense pain on the right side of
my abdomen and went to visit my personal doctor in San Antonio.
After undergoing an examination, I was immediately transported
by ambulance to the emergency department of Northeast Baptist
Hospital, where I underwent an emergency appendectomy
because my appendix had ruptured. I was accompanied by my
wife, Esmeralda, who stayed with me at the hospital for ten days
as I recuperated. After I was discharged, we hastily returned
home. During the next six months, I visited several doctors.
I experienced unbearable stomach bloating, pain, anxiety,
restlessness, and many sleepless nights. My body was emitting

signals I was unable to comprehend. Something was wrong, but I had no idea of its magnitude or what I was about to confront.

On December 31, 2018, after I'd been struggling for days with extreme stomach pain, my eldest son, Aurelio Matthew, drove me to a local hospital's emergency department for observation. My gut clenched and nausea overtook me as I feared the worst. A couple of hours passed, then I received the most dreadful news. The emergency doctor declared, "It does not look good. You have a lot of white spots all over your stomach. I believe it could be cancer."

The C-word, the word everyone fears: *cancer!*

Yes, cancer, one of life's deadliest diseases and one that does not discriminate. Cancer takes an innocent person and makes them its prisoner.

The doctor immediately gave me a referral to a local colorectal surgeon, Dr. Jaime L. Mayoral.

Aurelio Matthew turned around and embraced me. He said, "Pops, you are going to be just fine."

Our short drive back home felt endless. I was trying to catch my breath, which anxiety was trying to prevent me from doing. I was still in disbelief and in awe. *What am I going to do? Am I going to die or survive? How am I going to tell my wife, our youngest son, and my other family members?*

I did not believe the doctor's evaluation. In my mind, he was wrong with his initial assessment. I simply did not accept it. In total denial, I became full of dread and fear, my body trembling.

What would be my outcome? As nervousness and fear overtook me, I became clammy and teary-eyed. Many questions cluttered my mind.

Days later, I met with Dr. Mayoral and underwent examinations (a colonoscopy, X-rays, a sonogram, etc.). After receiving the results of these procedures, the doctor declared, "You have cancer, and you are going to need surgery soon." I stared at him, speechless. My wife did her best to console me, but

I was stunned and horrified. I felt as if I had run into a brick wall. My world had come to a complete stop. I was there, filling in a big void. What a waste! My wife did all the talking from then on.

Appointments were set for additional tests to be conducted within the next few days. I could not acknowledge anything. I sat there with a blank stare, no motor responses, and no thoughts. I was in a big black hole with no exit. A total void overtook me. My heart sank as I was shaken to the core.

I endured another long drive back home. This time, I was trying to hold on to my senses, trying not to lose it emotionally in front of my wife. I sat there solemnly and shook my head from side to side, thinking of the worst outcome: death.

I had to stay strong! There was nothing else for me to say.

After arriving home, I walked alone to the backyard. There I stood gazing at the sky with tears streaming down my cheeks as if in a downpour. I was sobbing loudly and pleading to God in agony, "Why me? Why me?!"

I kept pleading to Him, "Why this cancer, and why now? What did I do wrong to deserve this? Is it my past sins? What is it? I do not deserve this!?

I felt dejected, abandoned, and hopeless. My mind swirled around and around like waves crashing on the shore. I held back my tears, and a somber silence enveloped me.

I pled, "God, please help me! Help me! Help me! Forgive me for my sins!" Then I dropped to my knees and sobbed and sobbed, totally dejected. There was no future for me. What about my wife and kids? Who would take care of them? How would they support themselves? These and other questions raced through my convoluted mind as I kept crying.

Then I stood and began pacing back and forth in the backyard, trying to catch my breath. I was pacing back and forth, back and forth, with no end in sight.

The fear and anxiety began to overwhelm me. I continued crying. I was shaking frantically and had an uncontrollable urge to run away, to run to some other place where I could be alone and at peace with no issues whatsoever, no sickness, no disease, and no problems. I felt a burning desire to start a new life with a new identity and no medical problems. But reality kicked in, and again I cried uncontrollably. I feared death as I continued praying to God for a solution to this dreadful disease, but no answer came. I was all alone, facing agony and cancer, a deadly disease; was in fear for my life; and feared that I was losing my senses. Again I felt the urge to run away. But where would I go? What would I do?

I still questioned God: "Why me? Why now? I have my whole lifetime ahead of me." But there was no answer. All I could hear was the wind blowing and the birds chirping in the trees.

I grasped my head with both my hands and soberly prayed to God. "Please, God, help me. Please help me. Please help me overcome this. Please heal me. I am all Yours. "I trust in You, God! I trust in You, God!"

That was the moment I humbly gave my life to God, surrendering totally to my Father. A sense of peace engulfed my entire body. I sighed a big sigh of relief as I calmed down.

After a while, I decided to go back into the house and confront my loved ones. With my head bowed, I somberly and gingerly walked into the kitchen. As I glanced upward at the pantry, I saw something! It hit me right between the eyes, a wooden sign with the inscription, "Trust in the Lord" from Proverbs 3:5. Wow! Amazing! I stared at it for a while and read it repeatedly. *Trust in the Lord! Trust in the Lord!* I stood there in awe and repeated the words in my mind again and again. Finally, I received a direct and unexpected message from God, His way of letting me know, "I am here with you." God was manifesting in His infinite way and asking me to put my total trust in Him and no one else. This was an amazing, humbling experience.

Then I turned around and walked over to the kitchen table, distinctly hearing the soft and tender voice of my late mother in my mind. In Spanish she was saying, "Do not lose your faith. Do not lose your faith, Son. Trust in God. He will help you. He will heal you." Her soothing voice repeated these words again and again. She said, "Trust in God. Do not lose your faith. Do not lose your faith."

My entire being became overwhelmed with a sense of calmness and peace. I felt more at ease as the anguish and pain began to subside. I leaned across the table and gently grasped the Holy Bible with both my hands, then I opened it and began to read two impressive scriptures.

The first scripture I read was Psalm 23, followed by Psalm 91. I directed my prayers to the Omnipotent One, our Almighty God whom we consider the Maker of heaven and earth, the Supreme Being and divine healer, my true Father!

The anguish, fear, and pain had vanished. I experienced a moment of joy and peace as I was finally able to accept the truth. I have cancer! One of humankind's deadliest diseases. A disease everyone dreads. A disease I would be battling one-on-one in the coming months.

During this extraordinary solitary moment, I totally embraced God. I gave my entire life to Him. I said to myself, *It will be His will and not mine. Whatever the consequences, I accept them, God. You are my hope. You are my healer. Do what You want with me. I am all Yours!* This was a total surrender to God. My life was now in His divine hands.

During the next few days, I continued reading the Bible and mentally preparing myself for the upcoming surgery. I filled my mind with positive thoughts and placed my total faith in God. I am now in His divine embrace receiving His omnipotent care. There is no better place to be.

On January 14, 2019, I underwent cancer surgery at Methodist Hospital, San Antonio, under the care of Dr. Mayoral and his staff. The surgery took longer than seven hours with the removal of the omentum (an apron of fatty tissue primarily designed to protect the abdomen), also known as the "policeman of the abdomen"; six inches of the large intestine; and an unspecified number of cancerous tumors.

After enduring hours under the knife, I awoke in a daze, hearing a female nurse's faint and tender voice. After an hour, I was transported to my room, where my wife met me. There I began to experience excruciating pain around the outside of my stomach. I peered downward and detected a long incision with close to forty staples aligned from my sternum to below my belly button. Also, an NG tube had been inserted into my right nostril, passing through the sinuses, going into the esophagus, and then going down into the stomach. There was also a catheter in my urethra. I was confused, in pain, weak, off-balance, and overcome with nausea. Reality kicked in!

What have I gotten myself into? This dreadful pain! Is it ever going to go away?

My mind was convoluted and bombarded with uneasy thoughts and questions. I would trust in the surgeons to answer these troubling questions about my cancer.

Pain medications such as Tylenol, morphine, and Dilaudid would take effect for a while and minimize the pain. Otherwise, the gnawing and persistent pain was unbearable as it enveloped my body. It brought tears to my eyes and made me feel afraid.

Four days after the operation, I took a turn for the worst. As I lay awake in bed at two o'clock in the morning, to my disbelief, I became frigid with the coldness overtaking my entire body. The chills! I began to tremble uncontrollably. The coldness was unbearable. I began shaking uncontrollably. I had trouble catching my breath and was afraid of choking. I frantically called my wife, who awoke and became alarmed. She instantly rang for a nurse.

I was sitting on the left side of the bed with my head slumped and leaning to one side. I became lightheaded and frail. The room was a blur in whitish and grayish colors, and a somber silence fell over everything.

I wanted to relinquish my life. This was the end of the road for me. I seriously believed this was true. I said to myself, *God, if this is it, I am ready to go. Take me now. I am exhausted. I cannot bear the pain. Make it go away.*

My eyes began fluttering, and I was having trouble keeping them open. The nurses immediately placed several warm blankets over my body. The bitter cold was overtaking me as I trembled convulsively. I felt the coldness deep in the core of my inner self.

I was about to close my eyes when suddenly I barely heard my wife' sweet voice saying, "Al, wake up! Wake up! Do not go to sleep. Honey, please wake up. Do not give up!" She lightly shoved me in the side as I drifted off. Minutes later, I faintly observed a group of nurses rushing into the room to help me out. I guess I had blacked out for an unknown period. I was unable to recall anything.

After the ordeal, my wife nervously mentioned that I had pulled out my NG tube and vomited all over the place. My body was convulsing and had swung into fight mode. Several nurses and specialists rushed into the room as my vital signs spiraled downward. They immediately placed me into the bathroom and showered me with icy water. Then, they cautiously placed me back in bed. The nurses immediately inserted a new NG tube. I was provided with an oxygen mask and medications. My wife exclaimed, "You were septic, and you went into shock! Your body was poisoning itself. You were nearly at the breaking point. Your body turned toward survival mode as you fought to survive."

Given my dreadful condition, I recalled none of it. But in my wife's eyes, it was a terrifying event, something she wished never to experience again. She honestly believed it was the end of my life. I saw the tears in her eyes, the fragile smile on her lips, and the worried expression on her face. The ordeal I just experienced had shaken her to the core.

As the days passed, I gradually built up strength and began to drink liquids and consume soft solid foods. I made it a priority to challenge myself. I firmly stood and walked every day for one to two hours. I was grateful for my wife and one of my great friends, Art Benavides, for being there at my side every step of the way during my twenty-three-day ordeal.

Esmeralda and Art inspired me to stand, walk, and not give up. Art would constantly tell me, "Come on, big Al, you can do it. Keep going on, and do not stop. We are here for you. God is by your side. I will help you out. You will be fine and get over this."

Art was amazing! He kept urging me on and at times cracked jokes. Both of us joked around with one of the medical specialists regarding my IVs. I commented, "Are you going to give me a T-bone steak with a salad and baked potato tonight and some dessert such as hot apple pie and ice cream?"

The specialist laughed it off and replied, "It will be ready within an hour for you, sir."

I admit there were some days that were unbearable. I thought of stopping, giving up, or endlessly staying in bed. But I had to rise up, be strong, and fight on. There was no other choice but to continue fighting, continue surviving, and trusting in God. I needed to keep the faith, stay focused, motivate myself, and maintain a positive mental attitude. My will to survive lit a burning fire inside me and gave me the strength to continue.

Esmeralda's and Art's moral support was outstanding. I am also grateful that my two sisters, Norma Leal Salinas and Sonia Leal Thompson, and their husbands visited me and provided me with support. It brought a smile to my face and made a big difference in my recuperation.

Prior to my discharge, Dr. Mayoral informed us that the surgery wasn't a total success. He was able to remove most of the cancer. To my amazement, he read the initial pathology report from the previous year's emergency appendectomy, which indicated I had stage 4 adenocarcinoma of the appendix and pseudomyxoma peritonea. This disturbing news had a devastating effect on my morale. I began sobbing with fear.

It was apparent that Dr. Mayoral was upset with the previous surgeon, who had withheld the pathology report from us. He apologized for his counterpart's error and lack of professionalism. He also recommended we contact MD Anderson Hospital in Houston for further evaluation with the possibility of chemotherapy and another surgery. My wife immediately contacted the hospital and provided them with all the documents they requested.

After my discharge, we drove the more than three long hours and arrived home to a wonderful welcome from my two sons and other relatives. Everyone was surprised and enjoyed seeing me. But the area around my stomach at times throbbed in pain, which was unbearable. I was taking tramadol and Tylenol with codeine three to four times a day to ease the pain.

For the next few days, a nurse came over and changed my bandages and checked my incision. After a week passed, I paid another visit to Dr. Mayoral' s office for the uncomfortable process of having the forty-five or so staples removed from my abdomen.

Unfortunately, I had lost approximately thirty-five pounds and now weighed two hundred fifteen pounds. I felt extraordinarily weak, my muscles had atrophied, and I had little strength. I awoke every morning with nausea and intense pain. The medications helped for a bit, but the pain continued round the clock, at times spiraling out of control. Sometimes I felt like madly scratching my arms and body or cutting myself with a knife just to redirect the pain.

It was time for me to rise to the occasion, focus, and recover my health. But more importantly, I needed to keep humbly praying to God to heal me.

I prepared my mind for the arduous road ahead by reading the Holy Bible along with two inspirational books by Norman Vincent Peale. This was no time to retreat. My primary inspiration was my total faith and trust in God, closely followed by my love for my wife and sons.

In March 2019, we traveled to Houston and met with doctors, including surgeons and a pathologist, at MD Anderson Hospital. I underwent various medical tests including blood work, and the results were returned pending further review. The staff at MD Anderson were also disappointed with the surgeon who had failed to provide me with the pathology report from my appendectomy, never mind his failure to disclose my condition. After further discussion, the staff told me and my wife that they would contact us at a later point with their conclusions.

I was facing three options, they told me, listed from best-case scenario to worst-case scenario as follows: (1) wait three to four months and then run more tests and do a second round of blood work, then examine the results; (2) begin chemotherapy right away via intravenous injection; and (3) undergo an intensive operation and HIPEC (hyperthermic intraperitoneal chemotherapy).

We drove back to San Antonio united in prayer, hoping for the best. Once home, I nervously paced back and forth in our living room, waiting either to hear dreadful news or see a beacon of hope. My insides churned, my head throbbed, and my body ached with pain. I was reaching the point of hopelessness.

Within two weeks, a doctor from MD Anderson Hospital contacted us. After the team had met and reviewed my pathology results and the results from all the other tests, they decided it would be best if I pursued HIPEC. I was not aware of what this medical procedure entailed, so my wife and I decided to do some research.

Dr. Fournier and one of his associates at MD Anderson described HIPEC as hypothermic intraperitoneal chemoperfusion, a cancer treatment where the abdominal cavity is filled with chemotherapy drugs and distilled water which have both been heated to around 104° Fahrenheit. The heat is why the procedure is known as "hot" chemotherapy. He mentioned that HIPEC would be performed after they had removed all the tumors or lesions from my abdominal area. He indicated that HIPEC worked best for patients like me whose cancers had spread to or were confined to the inner lining of the stomach. In addition, HIPEC was successfully used to treat cancer nodules or invisible (microscopic) cancer cells. The procedure had saved the lives of many patients. Dr. Fournier told us that HIPEC was also known as "shake and bake." His comments made me laugh and settled my nerves.

As the days passed, I immersed myself in reading the Bible, having developed an intense indescribable feeling and a passion for God, a burning desire you might call it. At times as I read the Bible, a sense of euphoria would overtake me. My total trust was in God and no one else. I had no time to worry about anything else in life. My battle with cancer was my top priority. I was about to embark on a life-changing journey and fight one-on-one against cancer. I had to stay strong and lay the groundwork for this endeavor.

I started by preparing myself mentally and physically for a life-threatening operation. My faith and trust in God were my key weapons of choice in my battle for survival. My wife was managing all our personal affairs and had contacted family members, close friends, and associates to ask them to pray for me. Prayer groups were assembled, and everyone began to pray for my health and healing.

On April 15, 2019, I underwent the intensive operation and HIPEC at MD Anderson. The life-threatening operation lasted for around twelve hours. I awoke in a slight daze from the anesthesia, and after a while I was transported to a recovery room. The doctors and nursing staff were professional and compassionate, and provided outstanding care.

I was delighted to see my wife standing at my side with a

big smile. She gently took my hand and uttered in a soothing voice, "I love you. You are going to be fine. We were all praying for you. Praise God."

I had five tubes inserted into my body: the NG tube, a urinary catheter, a tube inserted on either side of my ribs going into my lungs, and a tube inserted below my incision. I became anxious and desperately wanted to pull both tubes out of my lungs. Taking short breaths, I felt a tightness and pain in my chest that was unbearable. As I struggled to breathe, I was aware I had no other option but to endure the hardship and pain. I had to heal my body. The pain medications were the perfect remedy, but the effects were only brief. The pain would reemerge, bringing with it a burning sensation around my stomach. The pain began to haunt me as it came again and again. At times it was so bad that I would curl up in the fetal position.

The doctors voiced their concern about my heart rate, which was too high, between 125 and 138 beats per minute. It was as if I were competing in a footrace. The staff monitored me continuously, and the doctors increased the dose of my pain medication to pacify me.

Later in the day, Dr. Fournier came to check up on me. He smiled and told me that the "shake and bake" procedure was a success. I thanked him, but more importantly, I thanked God.

After two days passed, the two tubes inserted near my rib cage on each side were removed. It was painful, but what a relief! Another two more days and the urinary catheter was removed, which caused me sharp pain and to discharge a few droplets of blood. Yet this was another relief! But I was feeble and exhausted. The nurses continuously monitored my heart rate and saw that it was now below one hundred beats per minute.

The doctors, seeing that I had become dehydrated and anemic, prescribed an increase in intravenous fluids and two more pints of blood, which were delivered through a PICC line going straight to my heart. After a couple of days, I began to recover and regain some of my strength.

Four more days passed, and on my birthday, April 23, I received good news from the head nurse: they were going to remove the NG tube. Later in the day, after the NG tube had been removed, and I breathed a huge sigh of relief. I could breathe fresh air again through my nostrils. Wow! It was if a veil had been removed from my mind.

The nurses had another surprise for me: a small birthday cake and colorful balloons. I was totally amazed and enjoyed the moment, an unforgettably joyful and peaceful time. However, I was unable to taste the cake. Although the occasion was short-lived, it left an impression on me. The nurses there were compassionate, loving, and professional.

Later that night, I took a turn for the worse. I felt miserable, was nauseous, and began to vomit a greenish substance. The vomiting wouldn't stop. My body was trembling as fear began to overtake me. The main physician insisted they insert a new NG tube, this time while I was awake. I dreaded this procedure.

Early the following morning a nurse and one of the doctors began the arduous task of inserting the NG tube. On the first go, they had trouble inserting the tube into my right nostril, so they tried the left one, but that was a no-go too as it began to bleed.

Soon thereafter, they acquired a thinner, more flexible tube and finally inserted it into my right nostril, through my esophagus, and down into my stomach. Then all the ugly liquid began to flow out through it. What a gruesome experience. I will never forget it. It took them a total of seven attempts to successfully insert the NG tube into my right nostril. This unpleasant experience brought pain and discomfort, causing tears to stream down my cheeks. What a miserable ordeal! I wouldn't wish it on anyone. Of course, my wife, wanting no part of this, had previously slipped quietly out of the room.

The NG tube was another relief, albeit a slight one, as it is cumbersome to have a tube in your nostril that goes into your throat and then into your stomach. Anyone who has undergone this type of painful procedure will understand. It's grotesque and unpleasant.

There were times when I would feel apprehensive and turn clammy. Out of desperation, I'd want to yank out the NG tube, jump out of bed, and flee the room. Praise God, my wife was by my side to console me. She gently held my hand, hugged me, and calmed my anxiety. I had no other solution but to endure the process and forge ahead. The physical process of recovering was difficult enough, but the psychological aspect was even more intense. I overcame my fear and my sense of failure by focusing on God and my family. Nothing else mattered to me. My priority was to recover and be healthy.

Now I was presented with another grave medical problem: my stomach stopped functioning. It lay there dormant without movement like a dead battery. I was provided with medications to treat this, but they did nothing. Now I was sitting there like an old car in a run-down garage with a mechanic at work trying to spark my ignition. My lips and palate were dry as my urge to drink water or eat food had dissipated.

One of our close friends, Joel Saldana, a retired federal agent, and his wife, Maricela, visited us in the hospital. It was very nice to see them and hear their words of encouragement. And sometimes my sisters, other relatives, or friends would call me on the phone. The ones I cherish the most that made a great impact on me were the video calls from Sammy Gomez, his brother, and their parents, Hilario Gomez and Ileana Gomez, all of whom would provide me with words of encouragement. But most important of all was their prayers to God and Jesus Christ for my healing. Sammy would say, "Coach Al, I love you. Jesus loves you. You are going to be fine." (Sammy is a child with Down syndrome and a congenital heart disorder who beat the odds and survived. His story appears in chapter 5.) The prayers and words of encouragement I received from all these people enabled me to continue the arduous road to recovery after surgery.

Ten days passed and I was moved to another recovery room, this one located on the nineteenth floor. During my stay there, something happened that had a direct effect on my Christian views and strengthened my belief that God does indeed work in mysterious ways.

One afternoon, I was weak and in pain with no desire to get up, just wanting to lie in bed for a while. But my wife convinced me to get out of bed and accompany her to the second floor to get a sandwich and a cup of coffee. It felt like an endless walk to the elevators as I was pulling the medical pole with my IV alongside me. Before reaching the elevators, I glanced to my right, toward the men's bathroom, and stopped. A tall, burly man walked out of the restroom, greeted us, and stopped to talk. From his somber expression, it was obvious to both me and my wife that something was bothering him. He told us that his wife was struggling with cancer and had trouble eating and in pain. Unbeknownst to us, she was the patient in the room adjoining mine. To our amazement, she had been diagnosed with the same type of cancer I had in the same month and same year I had been diagnosed.

After hearing this story, my wife and I were baffled. My wife commented, "You see, God works in mysterious ways! He has a plan for each of us."

The burly man had one simple request for us: "Will you please visit her, pray over her, and give her some encouragement?" We agreed to fulfill his request and continued on our way to the elevators, then went down to the second floor. My wife and I stared at each other in disbelief. We had an eerie feeling about this strange encounter. Our meeting was no coincidence. We knew deep down that it was divine intervention. God had sent us His godly inspiration by the power of the Holy Spirit.

An hour later, we ascended to the nineteenth floor and

stopped in to visit our neighbor. We knocked on the door, which the burly male opened while smiling wide. My wife and I sat next to the bed where his wife lay. Her facial expression and her color made it obvious that she was suffering and in pain. My wife and I formally introduced ourselves and exchanged pleasant greetings, following this up by praying the Our Father and other prayers. I gently held the woman's hand and spoke some words of encouragement. The most important thing I told her was, "Trust in God, and do not give up. He is there for you. Continue praying." She smiled warmly and thanked us for being there with her. I turned and looked across the room. Her husband was standing there smiling and with tears flowing down his cheeks. They both thanked us before we departed.

Back in our own room, my wife exclaimed, "Don't you see it? That was all God. He was working through you to encourage her. It was the Holy Spirit at work. Honey, this is amazing!"

Mentally, I was drained. I started sobbing with tears streaming down my cheeks. I heartily thanked God for all His gracious blessings. Also, I prayed for my fellow patient, asking that He get her through her surgery and ensure her successful recovery. I knew that God had a plan and a purpose for me. I was not aware of His divine plan, but I accepted the fact of it. I was finally convinced that there are no coincidences in life! God is in control!

Sometimes we do not grasp this, only coming to understand it a later date or time. We must understand, everything happens according to God's timing, not ours. It is all about God's will, not ours.

On another occasion, I was alone in my hospital room as my lovely wife had left to go back to the apartment and get some rest. Lying in bed, I glanced toward the ceiling with tears running down my cheeks. My entire body was overtaken by a feeling of comfort. During this precious moment of peace and solitude, I began speaking directly to God.

"God, help me! I need Your help more than ever before. I trust in Thee, my Lord God. Please heal me. You are my salvation, dear Lord. I am Yours to do with as You please. Your will be done."

I continued speaking to God for a long time, then I dozed off. That night I slept long and peacefully, which was much needed.

After five or six hours, I awoke to find my wife sitting by my side with a smile on her face. This was the longest time I had ever slept in a hospital bed, which meant I had been comfortable for once.

Seeing as I was still in the hospital, I made it a priority to get out of bed and walk frequently. During my walks, I would encounter other patients and encourage them not to give up. More important than that was my encouraging them to have faith and trust in God.

After twenty-three days—quite an ordeal—I had successfully recovered and was finally discharged. Then my wife and I stayed in a hotel for a week waiting for a visit with my main surgeon, Dr. Fournier. My wife and I spent some precious moments together praying and having conversations with God. I love her deeply! Without her encouragement and love, I would never have made it through. I praise God for blessing me with a righteous and wonderful wife.

The follow-up examination with Dr. Fournier turned out great. My blood work showed no problems. A physician assistant cautiously removed the forty-eight or so staples from my stomach area. Then Dr. Fournier exclaimed to me, "You are NED [no evidence of disease]! There is no trace of the disease. You may go home now. We will be in contact and will see you again in six months."

This was the greatest news my wife and I had heard in months. She and I continually praised God and thanked Him on our drive back to San Antonio, where I began the grueling journey of healing from the surgery. The next few months provided me an opportunity to spend quality time with my wife and two sons, my having gained a deep appreciation for the things that are most important in life after God—my family, my friends, and my well-being.

I was scheduled for a follow-up exam in six months. As the date approached, I became apprehensive with sleepless nights. Fearing the worst, I asked myself, *Has the cancer returned?*

On November 2, 2019, my wife and I arrived in Houston, Texas, and rented a hotel room. During the night I became restless and anxious with thoughts racing in my mind. I had difficulty sleeping as I was imagining the worst. My wife came to my rescue with a tender hug, which calmed my nerves. We prayed and read passages from the Bible. Afterward, I felt more at ease.

Early the next morning, I underwent a CT scan and blood work at MD Anderson. It took another anxious day for the results to come back. Then we met with my surgeon Dr. Fournier, whose demeanor that day was pleasant and professional. He thoroughly reviewed the results with us and commented, "You are disease-free." Wow! I breathed a great sigh of relief. It felt as if a huge burden had just been lifted from my shoulders. My wife and I graciously thanked the doctor.

On our drive home, I recalled the words of an elderly woman from church who had endured many dreadful things in her life. She said, "Bad times, tough times, rough times, and sad times, no matter the circumstances, we must still have faith in God. He will always be there for us."

Yes, for a moment I had let doubt overtake me to the point that I doubted God's grace. But I embraced His compassion and love. I knew God was with me every step of the way. I praise God and thank Him daily for His merciful blessings! Sometimes I break down in tears when I realize how great God is.

I recalled a Bible verse where King David is addressing God,

Psalm 107:6, which reads, "Then they cried to the Lord in their trouble, and he delivered them from their distress."

My last follow-up visit at MD Anderson Hospital was in April 2022. I had more blood work and had a CT scan. This visit revealed the amazing fact that I was still disease-free. Praise God!

I said a special word of thanks to everyone whose prayers had enabled me to deal with this stressful and challenging time of battling cancer. Their thoughts and prayers made an enormous difference, as did God's love and tender mercies.

This remarkable experience caused me to have a change of heart and to place my faith and trust in God. I believe that God allows adversity to enter our lives because it enables us to get closer to Him and love Him. God has a plan for each one of us. We must accept His plan and not fight against it. God is in control! The most important thing of all is to trust in Him! God loves us dearly and desires that we come closer to Him.

Other people in life are currently going through the same ordeal as I, battling cancer. Several friends are undergoing chemotherapy for breast cancer, stomach cancer, throat cancer, and prostate cancer, among other cancers. I pray for them all and wish them a safe and speedy recovery.

No one ever said that life would be easy and we would never encounter any challenges or difficulties.

Life is bittersweet! It is a long journey for everyone. And the journey can be fulfilling and joyful or sparse and dreadful.

Many of my friends and family seek to live our lives one day at a time, enjoying ourselves to the utmost, not worrying about anything or anyone or what tomorrow might bring. A few of my friends have expressed the desire to travel all over the United States and the world. Our new generation of young adults seek to enjoy life to the utmost by playing video games and partying— enjoying the now and not worrying about tomorrow or what the future might bring.

Other people, by contrast, walk a more difficult, unhappier path in life. They struggle to earn enough money to meet their basic needs and are in debt with personal loans, car payments, insurance premiums, student loans, credit card payments, and medical bills, among other things. And they are embroiled in other serious matters such as trying to revive a failing marriage, care for a sick or troubled child, and reduce the amount of stress at home and work. They may also have health problems or even a disability. Such people are unfortunately stuck in a rut and are stressed out to the point of depression.

Many people use, and sometimes abuse, alcoholic beverages and narcotics to alleviate their pain and suffering. Some people even contemplated moving far away, leaving everyone and everything they know behind, and embarking on a new life. Still others consider a more sinister route, the worst-case scenario, suicide.

How do we as people deal with all the issues that overwhelm us and suck the joy from our lives, drastically affecting our health? There are many ways to answer this question. We have many options.

Do we merely confide in a family member or close friend, or do we visit a psychologist or psychiatrist and possibly take prescription medication to alleviate or at least mask our anguish and pain?

Or is there another viable solution, something more promising and easier?

Life has its difficulties. We must keep moving forward nevertheless. Yes! But in what direction do we travel, and under whose guidance?

I completely agree with something my late maternal grandmother, Janie, said: "When faced with overwhelming odds, place your full faith and trust in God. No one else is going to be there for you, but God will."

Who else in the world is omnipotent, divine, and all knowing and has infinite knowledge and power? None other than the Almighty God, the Maker of heaven and earth! Our heavenly Father is whom we must confide in and trust. We must make the decision to change our lives for the better when we are faced with adversity and challenges.

Lucille Ball, the comedienne and television icon, faced some tough challenges and endured hardships such as a failed marriage, miscarriages, and ruthless criticism. But that didn't stop her from moving forward in life. She developed a unique character and became a success on the show *I Love Lucy*.

God has gifted each one of us with free will, allowing us to make our own choices and pursue our own paths in life. It is our choice to either trust God or reject Him, to either continue struggling in life and feeling pain or find relief and peace through God.

Bear in mind we are part of the United States, an independent country, one nation under God. Most Americans accept this, knowing that we are a Christian nation.

Our Founding Fathers acknowledged and paid tribute to God, referring to Him by different names including Almighty God, God Almighty, the Creator, divine providence, the Almighty Being, Lord, the Supreme Being, and the Supreme Judge, among others.

One of the most famous founders of our nation is George Washington, a devoted Christian and man of prayer who displayed immense faith in God. His mother ministered him to trust in God and never to forget it. George heeded the counsel of his beloved mother for the rest of his life and became a famous general in the American Revolution. His prayer at Valley Forge for God's divine help left an impression on many Americans. After his success fighting in the American Revolution, he became the first president of the United States.

President George Washington, in his Thanksgiving Proclamation of October 3, 1789, said, "Whereas it is the duty of all nations to acknowledge the providence of Almighty God, to obey his will, to be grateful for his benefits, and humbly to implore his protection and favor."[1]

On July 30, 1956, President Dwight D. Eisenhower signed legislation establishing "In God We Trust" as the motto of the United States. Prior to this, "In God We Trust" was inscribed on US coins and bills. The first federal coin was the two-cent coin, minted in 1864 with the inscription "In God We Trust."

Today, if you check your wallet and look at each bill—$100, $50, $20, $10, $5, and $1—you will find on the back of each the inscription "In God We Trust." The phrase is also inscribed on the front of all United States coins.

When we say "In God we trust," we can think of it simply as having trust in God.

Do we trust God only when things go wrong? Or do we try to place the blame on others, or the community, or society in general? Blaming others is not going to solve our problems. We must face reality! We should not cave in!

Exclusively trust in Him, Almighty God, the God of love and miracles! He will always be there for us. We must seek Him earnestly and open our hearts to Him in total devotion.

God is referred to by different names in the Bible. Each name has its own meaning and conveys its own power. One of these names is Jehovah Rapha, the Great Physician, who heals the physical bodies and emotions of His people. (This name brings much comfort and hope to those who have prayed for healing and deliverance from disease, illness, brokenness, or painful circumstances. It reminds us all that God accepts that we need His help. He understands we are all in need of healing, and He promises to redeem us and repair every broken place in our lives.)

In Mark 14:1, Jesus Christ confronted His disciples and told them, "Let not your hearts be troubled. You believe in God; believe also in me" (NIV).

There is no one else in whom to put your total faith and trust. God will get you through your troubled times. Believe in Him. Several months ago, I accompanied my wife and mother-in-law, Leopolda "Pola" Martinez, to visit a lifelong friend of theirs in Pharr, Texas. Their friend, Irma Chapa, who was elderly and had been suffering from cancer for more than three years, was originally diagnosed with breast cancer, for which she underwent chemotherapy and had one of her breasts surgically removed. Now, thanks to the grace of God, she was free of cancer! She was an ecstatic bell ringer for cancer survivors.

Prior to arriving at Ms. Chapa's residence, I saw a tractor trailer about two vehicle lengths ahead of us while we were waiting in traffic. In the back window of the cab were large bold letters reading, "In God We Trust." I found this odd and was bewildered by it. Was this a special revelation or something else unbeknown to me?

While en route to Ms. Chapa's residence, Pola related that she had spoken to Ms. Chapa two days prior and that she sounded tired and seemed delusional. Pola was distraught and disturbed by Ms. Chapa's fragile condition. Unfortunately, the cancer had returned and spread to Ms. Chapa's brain, and it was having a serious effect on her cognition. She had trouble speaking and recognizing people.

Pola said that Ms. Chapa had mentioned seeing her own husband a handful of times over the past few days. This was amazing as he had been deceased for more than eight years. Ms. Chapa indicated she had also observed four or five more of her deceased family members, including Pola's husband who had passed twelve years ago.

My wife and I mentally prepared ourselves for the visit. When we arrived at Ms. Chapa's residence, we were greeted by several of her family members. We saw Ms. Chapa lying in a small bed located in a corner of the family room. She appeared discolored and frail and was covered with several blankets.

There was a medium-gray scarf covering her head, and she easily recognized us. We exchanged greetings and hugged her.

Ms. Chapa asked how my mother was doing. I replied, "As usual, she is doing fine." Ms. Chapa recalled having seen her several months ago leaving the hospital when she herself was being admitted. As I sat close to Ms. Chapa, she again mentioned seeing my mother leaving the hospital while she, Ms. Chapa, was being admitted. They had exchanged greetings with one another. It was eerie to hear of this; it caused me to shiver and gave me goose bumps. Unbeknownst to Ms. Chapa, my mother had passed away at least seven years prior.

Ms. Chapa thanked me for the deer meat I previously had given her. It was a ritual of mine to provide her with some venison each year after I harvested a whitetail buck.

Ms. Chapa later made fun of her dear friend Pola and asked how her husband Robert was doing. Pola answered, "He is doing fine and misbehaving as usual." Ms. Chapa smiled but appeared to be in pain, slightly grasping for air. It should be noted that my father-in-law, Robert, passed away more than eight years before this.

She exclaimed, "I thank God for giving me a life and a second chance to live my life in the United States! He blesses me. I trust in God."

My wife gently held Ms. Chapa's hand and silently prayed for her. Ms. Chapa smiled as tears rolled down her cheeks. She quietly uttered, "You have a gift from God. Keep praying for others. I have lived an amazing life, and my time is drawing to a close." My wife graciously thanked her, appearing to have been humbled by those kind words.

Ms. Chapa gazed grimly at me and uttered, "Trust in Him and continue with your faith!"

The three of us were deeply moved by her. We all cried somberly and stared at each other. We knew her time was short. Knowing that her journey on earth was ending, all three of us were saddened by her frail physical condition. We prayed to God for peace and healing.

We later said our final farewell to Ms. Chapa and her family members. Then we departed the residence and slowly drove out of the neighborhood. I saw an incoming white pickup truck with bold letters above the front windshield reading, "In God We Trust."

I was amazed! This was the second time in two hours I had seen the same message. I gazed over at my wife and told her what I had seen. I knew deep within me that it was an indirect message from God. My wife commented, "It is all God's work. He is communicating with you."

I became emotional and wept, pulling the vehicle to the side of the road so I could compose myself. I was cognizant that our almighty God was again at work.

Further evidence of this appears in scripture: "So is my word that goes out from my mouth: It will not return to me empty but will accomplish what I desire and achieve the purpose for which I sent it" (Isaiah 55:11 NIV).

Sadly, a week later, we were notified that Ms. Chapa had died. She is now at peace with God, her husband, and her other departed members. We miss her dearly.

As you go on in life with its daily struggles, don't forget to lend a helping hand to those who are less fortunate than you and pray for them. Also, minister the Word of God and teach people that there is always Someone out there willing to help them out. Most importantly, you should keep the faith, constantly pray, and above all trust in God Almighty and our Lord and Savior Jesus Christ.

My late aunt Lucy, who succumbed to breast cancer, phrased it this way: "Always trust in God's love and power. He is always there to help you out. God wants you to place Him first in your life. God wants your total confidence and trust in Him. Always pray to God no matter the circumstance, be it good or bad. Let God take over your life."

Only God knows what lies ahead in our lives, including the challenges and struggles we'll face seeking to succeed in life and draw closer to Him. God desires only the best for us. He loves us and has formed us in His own image.

We must trust in God and hold onto our faith! We must keep moving ahead in life, taking one step at a time, not being selfish, but helping others along the way, especially those in need, those who are less fortunate, and those with disabilities.

CHAPTER 2

KEEPING THE FAITH

The Lord preserves the faithful.

—Psalm 31:23 (AMP)

Each year, cancer strikes thousands of innocent people in the United States and all over the world. It does not discriminate based on race, gender, religion, or nationality. Many of the people who are stricken with cancer unfortunately do not survive this deadly disease, whereas others take the long and treacherous path of battling the disease and hoping to survive. Whatever route these people choose, their lives change drastically and forever.

There are more than two hundred distinct types of cancers, characterized by abnormal cell growth. There are also many different causes, ranging from radiation, to chemicals, to viruses, to environmental exposure.

According to the American Cancer Society, during 2021 the top five deadliest cancers, listed in order from the deadliest on down, are as follows:

1) lung cancer
2) colorectal cancer
3) pancreatic cancer

4) breast cancer

5) prostate cancer.

The American Cancer Society also estimated the number of new cancer cases in the United States in 2021 to be around 1.9 million, having expected 608,570 Americans to die of cancer in 2021. They posit that the top three deadliest cancers are female breast, prostate, and lung. Cancer is considered the second most common cause of death in the US, surpassed only by heart disease. It is estimated one in three people will be diagnosed with cancer in their lifetime.[1]

Besides proper medical care, cancer patients require emotional support from family members, friends, coworkers, and/or support groups. The emphasis should be on prayer and one's own deep-rooted faith to continue moving forward in life—an unwavering and absolute faith!

Faith is having a firm belief in something for which there is no proof. Plain and simple, faith is a belief and complete trust in God.

The gospels teach us about enthusiastic faith. "But without faith it is impossible to please him: for he that cometh to God must believe that he is, and that he is a rewarder of them that diligently seek him" (Hebrews 11:6).

You must trust God because He cares about you and your life. He has a plan for you just as He does for each and every one of us. He loves you and wants you to draw closer to Him and His Son Jesus Christ.

Ephesians 2:8 tells us, "For it is by grace you have been saved, through faith" (AMP).

Amazing! You read it! Through faith! Yes, faith! Believe and you shall be healed! The main ingredient is faith. Passionately believe, and by the grace of God you will have excellent results.

My mother-in-law, Leopolda Martinez, age seventy-eight, is a living example of a loving person with a tremendous amount of faith who has fought cancer. At the age of thirty-six, she was diagnosed with uterine cancer and was subsequently hospitalized for surgical removal of the cancerous tumor and a hysterectomy. Doctors prescribed a number of medications, which she took for several months leading up to her being disease-free. Leopolda proclaimed, "What kept me going in life was constant prayer and my total trust and faith in God."

This was one of several heart-wrenching experiences she'd had in her life. Years prior to this ordeal, she lost her first son at the age of six years to an accidental gunshot to the neck. He lived for a few months after being shot, then passed. Then she underwent two divorces and became a single parent, faced with the dilemma of raising six children (three boys and three girls).

Years later, she was struck another devastating blow when her son Luis Antonio died of AIDS at the tender age of thirty. But Leopolda kept going on and trusting in God's plan for her life.

She once told me, "God has a plan for everyone, and there is a reason I am still alive today. No matter what happens to me in life, nothing will ever separate me from God's love."

In 2019, Leopolda faced yet another ordeal: cancer. Her diagnosis was skin cancer (melanoma) on the left cheek of her face. Melanoma strikes thousands of Americans every year.

Leopolda began treatments and later underwent successful facial reconstruction surgery. She received other treatments and took prescription medications for the next several months. According to the doctors, there was no more evidence of the disease in her body. Leopolda was elated with the doctor's news. She immediately thanked God for His good grace and blessings.

Several weeks later, I was alone with Leopolda at the dinner table and spoke to her about life in general. She smiled cheerfully and stated, "Life is never easy. We have our ups and downs. We must learn how to face our challenges and continue on. But the important thing to remember is that God will always be there for me and you. Seek Him out and keep praying. Do not lose faith, and most importantly, trust in Him."

As Leopolda continued her journey, I noticed that she set aside about an hour each morning to pray and embrace God's everlasting love. A family woman devoted to prayer! A woman devoted to God!

Those were very encouraging words to hear from this strong woman with unwavering faith who has endured many hardships in life. I am forever thankful for her priceless advice.

I also recall the reassuring words of a Catholic nun: "One must have great faith to receive remarkable results. Many people have little or no faith and expect positive results. It is your enormous faith which will provide infinite results."

What greater way to show your faith than to surrender to God totally and trust in Him. God is a Spirit, eternal, infinite, with the power and the wisdom to create life. He is filled with love, truth, and holiness.

Yes, God is the omnipotent Supreme Being, a God we must worship in spirit as noted in the Holy Scriptures. John 4:24 reads, "God is a spirit: and they that worship him must worship him in spirit and in truth."

By performing this amazing symbol of your faith, He will heal you and help you get through the difficult challenges you face.

We must choose to have faith even though we face numerous obstacles in life. We are tested sometime or another in our lives. How we respond to these challenges determines the lives we will lead.

When we get knocked down, we can either stay there on the ground and give up or stand back up and fight on. We must continue moving forward.

Some people say life has not been fair to them, that they have been cursed and suffer from bad luck. Perhaps they haven't come to terms with the fact that life is not easy. Everyone on earth will face some sort of catastrophe or other. At such times, we must have faith and believe in God.

And some people, like me, experience firsthand struggle a disease or disability or some other setback. My cancer diagnosis was life-changing in that it altered my outlook in life and led me to seek God and get closer to Him.

In the end, it is conviction and faith that keeps us going on, struggling to survive so we can continue to enjoy precious time with our loved ones.

We must intensify our faith through prayer because it is our faith that will move us closer to God.

Consider the glorious promise that Jesus Christ made to his disciples in Mark 11:22–24: "Have faith in God. Truly I tell you, if anyone says to this mountain, 'Go, throw yourself into the sea,' and does not doubt in their heart but believes that what they say will happen, it will be done for them. Therefore I tell you, whatever you ask for in prayer, believe that you have received it, and it will be yours."

Yes! Our true Father! The one and only living God! The Supreme Being who loves us unconditionally. Let us focus on God and believe in Him. Surrender to God and let Him take possession of our lives. God loves us and will bless us.

Stephanie Wilson is a close friend of ours from Laguna Vista, Texas, who has great faith in God. She is the founder of the Lower Valley Event Committee, an organization which organizes adaptive social events for children and young adults with disabilities. Currently she is the program director of the nonprofit named Big Heroes located in Brownsville, Texas, whose vision is to create a God-centered environment, empowering young adults with special needs to be recognized for their contributions to an inclusive community. Stephanie commented, "The name Big Heroes is a short form of Believe in God's Heroes."

Stephanie is the proud mother of Jason, an eighteen-year-old adult with several disabilities. She has a strong faith in God and an extreme love for her son. During our telephone conversation, she provided me with her son's remarkable timetable.

Jason Wilson was born in 2001 at a hospital in Portland, Oregon, a healthy eight-pound, ten-ounce baby boy with a full head of hair. Within the first week, he contracted jaundice. Stephanie indicated, "We followed the doctor's orders and underwent several tests. But his condition worsened after a week, and we subsequently took him to another pediatrician, who diagnosed him with advanced-stage jaundice."

Stephanie noted, "The doctors initially misdiagnosed Jason, and his elevated levels of bile from the jaundice affected his brain. He would scream twelve hours a day as his brains were being fried." A growth chart used by a pediatrician revealed Jason's weight was low (he was skinny) and his body was small for his age. However, he had a huge head, in the nineteenth percentile.

After Jason had turned nine months old, he was taken to another hospital and other specialists for examinations. They ran different tests and determined that something was wrong with him but provided no diagnosis, still unable to determine his exact medical condition.

At fifteen months old, like any other normal child, Jason began to walk and speak small words such as *mom* and *dad* and his own name. Unfortunately, after he was vaccinated as mandated by the government, his life changed drastically. He became nonverbal, never speaking a word or making any sound at all.

Stephanie declared, "Jason stopped talking, and his mannerisms diminished. He changed for the worse and at times had a faraway look in his eyes as if in a daze. He made zero eye contact and was in his own world." A few years later, Stephanie became aware that the vaccinations had affected Jason's mind and well-being. She researched the topic and became a true believer and an opponent of mandatory vaccinations (i.e., and antivaxxer) for children.

Jason didn't utter a single word until he was more than four years old. Stephanie made sure he received the proper medical care and enrolled him in both physical and speech therapy. He was thereafter officially diagnosed with cerebral palsy. Jason continued with his therapies, but with minor results. He would constantly be drooling without any interaction and a floppy body with no muscle tone.

In her desperation, Stephanie decided to try alternative options besides regular medications. She contacted a cousin in Switzerland who provided her with several homeopathic remedies for Jason. After Stephanie had given Jason a dose, it proved beneficial to his health, causing him to gain weight and make progress. Another dose resulted in Jason no longer drooling. Stephanie was elated and claimed, "Jason began to emerge and come alive, communicating with us, from no words and no communication to saying whole strings of words. It was truly a miracle! Jason has changed and is able to develop and is more engaged."

Unfortunately, Jason was later diagnosed with autism, a neurological disability he had not been born with.

During this time, the family was living in the state of Washington, and because of the cold, wet climate, they decided to relocate to South Texas. Being in the warmer weather and being outdoors was a better environment for Jason.

Stephanie recalls the first time Jason tried to step onto the sand at the beach in South Padre Island. He was terrified and overly cautious. The new environment and the sand's texture were overwhelming, causing sensory overload for him. It took Jason awhile to get accustomed to the feeling of the sand and walking on it barefoot. Stephanie always made it a priority to take Jason outside the house and involve him in extracurricular activities. She did not want to limit him.

I questioned Stephanie about her faith in relation to her son's disability. She commented, "Jason is a person just like you and me. God made him perfect. I have tremendous faith in God. I do not view Jason as a person with a disability but instead as a person with a gift. God made him in accordance with His plan."

Stephanie continued, "I have always helped Jason to be the best he could be. It has changed our lives for the better. I can see God's plan through the pain we have experienced. He is such a blessing. I am aware Jason interprets life differently from the way we do."

Stephanie recalled a dream she had several years ago. "I was in heaven with Jason, and we were both able to have a regular conversation like two adults. He had no disability and appeared like a normal person. I was amazed and began to cry. I love him immensely."

Stephanie placed Jason in special education classes and obtained a one-on-one personal aid for his safety. Jason has a hard time focusing and finds verbal concepts confusing. Every year he makes improvements little by little. The therapies have helped him function better.

According to Stephanie, Jason was thirteen years old—an opportune time—when the door opened for him to attend a prom in Brownsville, Texas, an event hosted by a local church supporting special needs children and young adults from the community. It was evident Jason enjoyed himself, the music, and the whole experience. Stephanie was overwhelmed with joy and soon became involved with the Lower Valley Event Committee, which grew over time and expanded throughout the community and into other areas.

Once he turned eighteen, Jason could understand basic concepts, but he still needed to work on his social skills. Stephanie took the initiative and created several adaptive sports programs, such as baseball, soccer, and basketball, for special needs kids in her community. She commented, "There was no pressure put on them and nothing but baby steps for them to take." I also advocated for the kids in our school district.

Several years ago, Stephanie met my wife, who was the executive director of the Capable Kids Foundation, and developed a friendship. Thus, she signed Jason up to play adaptive football. After her relationship with my wife had flourished, Stephanie and her organization joined in and came under the umbrella of the Capable Kids Foundation in the Lower Rio Grande Valley. She provided additional resources and extracurricular activities for the special needs community in her area.

"It was hard balancing a family with three teenagers, including Jason," Stephanie said. I left my career as a group leader at a direct sales company to care for Jason. He was my priority."

Stephanie exclaimed, "We have to put our kids first in life and sacrifice. What kept me going is my personal experience with Jason, which keeps me motivated. It has shown me that my purpose in life is to serve those with special needs, which fills my life with joy. It is my immense faith in God and the love I have for Jason and my family that keeps me going."

During the coronavirus pandemic with the curfew and stay-at-home orders, Stephanie began assisting Jason with teletherapy. He and others participated in distance learning three days a week for schoolwork, including a workout video. This process enabled them to stay connected to our charity and provided them with an avenue to have fun. These kids and young adults were desperate to go back to school and be with their friends and learn. According to Stephanie, many special needs students were isolated all day at home with nothing to do and became sad and depressed. They needed to socialize with others and enjoy themselves. She always makes it a priority to keep Jason busy and properly accommodate him with the right tools, including during the lockdowns.

What an amazing story and impressive situation thanks to the faith and loving devotion of a mother.

This is merely a small window into what other parents and

other people have endured in life with their loved ones. They hold their ground with a strong faith in God!

Ephesians 2:8 states, "For it is by grace you have been saved, through faith—and this is not from yourselves, it is the gift of God" (NIV).

Many stories in the Bible depict great faith exhibited by different individuals. Some people begged Jesus Christ to heal them or a loved one from infirmity. The ultimate request Jesus received was to raise a beloved family member from the dead. Jesus complied and miraculously raised Lazarus, the daughter of Jairus, and the son of the widow at Nain.

One story in the Bible stands out among the others. It is about a certain woman who demonstrates monumental faith in Jesus, resulting in her complete healing.

This woman was plagued with a blood issue for twelve years. She was in pain and had suffered at the hands of many physicians. Instead of getting better, her health grew worse. She had spent all her money so the doctors could heal her. Unfortunately, she was in dire straits, in distress, and out of options.

The woman had heard of Jesus's miracles performed on people with disabilities, people who were sick, and people who were dead. She sought Jesus out from among the crowd, believing she would be healed. Mark 5:28 says, "For she said, If I may touch but his clothes, I shall be whole."

The woman was certain that if she touched the hem of Jesus's garment, she would be healed. She fought the crowd surrounding Jesus and touched His garment. Jesus immediately felt a release of power. He turned and asked who had touched Him.

The woman, afraid, was trembling. She knew something had miraculously transpired inside her body. She came to Jesus and humbly knelt before Him, then told Him the truth of her suffering. He exhibited compassion and love, and He said to her, "Daughter, thy faith hath made thee whole; go in peace and be whole of thy plague" (Mark 5:34).

During this brief encounter, Jesus acknowledged the woman's intense faith in Him. Her belief made her whole, or shall I say healthy. Her solemn faith prevailed, ultimately determining the power and the blessing she received. God graciously compensated her.

There are other stories of faith in the Bible concerning sick people whom Jesus's miraculous power healed. In Matthew 9:28–29, Jesus encountered two blind men who followed Him and sought mercy. Jesus asked them if they believed He could heal them. They replied yes. As noted in Matthew 9:29, Jesus gently touched their eyes and said, "According to your faith be it unto you." Miraculously their eyes were opened and they could see. Faith had overcome fear and disbelief! Here faith is demonstrated as having unmeasurable power over sickness, demon possession, and death.

We must firmly hold onto our faith in our hearts, minds, spirits, and souls.

Another example of a person with steadfast faith is Mother Teresa. In 1979, she was awarded the Nobel Peace Prize for her outstanding work in services to charity and the impoverished.

Mother Teresa spoke five different languages and was one of the most famous missionaries in the world. She was well-known for her love and compassion toward the homeless and less fortunate, the poorest among society. She wholeheartedly served God and dedicated her entire life to assisting the poor.

Most people are not aware there were times Mother Teresa was plagued by pain and doubt. In September 1946, she was on a train during her annual retreat and heard the voice of Christ. She later called it a "second calling" or a "call within a call." During this calling, the voice told her to go to India to serve the poorest of the poor. She obeyed and went on to do a great amount of charitable work supporting children and orphanages.

Several years later, in 1950, Mother Teresa founded the Missionaries of Charity located in Calcutta, India. Her tremendous faith and trust in God were evident in her unselfish service to others less fortunate. She is considered by many as one of the most generous and influential individuals the world has ever seen. Mother Teresa's lifelong generosity, love, and kindness was evident in her faithful service to God and to people stricken with poverty.

Years after her death, in 2016 the Catholic Church canonized Mother Teresa as Saint Teresa of Calcutta.

As previously mentioned, our faith in God and our Lord and Savior Jesus Christ is what keeps us going in life. It is a faith we cannot ever see or touch—an immeasurable faith without end.

Hebrews 11:1 says, "Now faith is the substance of things hoped for, the evidence of things not seen."

We must continue to pursue faith and to hold it deep within our hearts so that it becomes a faith no one can take away from us. Let us strongly believe in this faith and cling to it so we can continue our wonderful journey through life. It is this absolute faith that will heal us!

Furthermore, as we continue on our unwavering faith, let us continue trusting in God.

CHAPTER 3

UNCONDITIONAL LOVE

> *For ye yourselves are taught of God to love one another.*
>
> —1 Thessalonians 4:9

Many individuals live their lives without knowing the true meaning of love. They live in solitude with no one to share their lives with, never experiencing real love for another person.

We may ask ourselves, what is love? Where does one find it? How can I get it? Can people live without it? These are only a handful of the questions philosophers and other human beings have asked for centuries. Many of us have never experienced love, while others have encountered it in a most profound way, a deep-rooted love that penetrates their heart, mind, body, and soul, a burning desire deep within, engulfing their entire lives! Several people have described falling in love as losing one's breath or skipping a heartbeat.

The topic of love is mentioned numerous times in the Bible. Love is one of the most important and one of the greatest emotions one can have toward others. Without it, one is hollow inside and empty inside, lonely, miserable, and numb—a dark place with a void.

Who was the greatest teacher of all time concerning the

subject of love? None other than our Lord and Savior Jesus Christ. His main teachings consistently stressed that we love one another.

The Bible dedicates a section solely to love (the Excellence of Love) in 1 Corinthians 13:2–3: "But [if I] do not have love I am nothing. If I give all my possessions to feed the poor, and if I surrender my body to be burned, but do not have love, it does me no good at all" (AMP).

There is also the gloriously declaration in 1 Corinthians 13:13, "And now these three remain: faith, hope, and love. But the greatest of these is love" (NIV).

Wow! How amazing is that? The greatest of these is love. Excellent! What more can one ask for!

We must understand that there is Someone who cares for us and loves us dearly. God is the One who embraces us with love.

How can we doubt God's love for us when He gave up His only begotten Son, Jesus Christ, as the ultimate sacrifice for the forgiveness of our sins? Christ suffered immensely under the hands of the Roman soldiers who brutally beat him to a pulp. This culminated in the greatest worldly sacrifice and sacred gift to humanity: the crucifixion and death of Christ and His miraculous resurrection. The gospel proclaims, "For God so loved the world, that He gave His only begotten Son, that whosoever believeth in Him should not perish, but have everlasting life" (John 3:16 NIV).

Love is also written of in 1 Corinthians 13:7: "Love bears all things (regardless of what comes), believes all things (looking for the best in each one), hopes all things (remains steadfast during difficult times), and endures all things (without weakening)" (AMP).

One of the world's most famous writers, William Shakespeare, wrote a play about the tragic love of two young lovers from Italy known as Romeo and Juliet who were part of two powerful feuding families who had a long-running vendetta. This young and innocent couple experienced love at first sight when they first met. Their overpowering love and passion for one another superseded all other loyalties. *Romeo and Juliet* is the epitome of a love story, showing that love totally engulfs a person's emotions. Unfortunately, this love story culminated in the tragic death of the two protagonists. Their romantic love was described in many ways. It was breathtaking and bright.

Although Romeo and Juliet are considered by many to be the world's most famous lovers, there were other memorable couples with moving experiences, for example, Cleopatra and Mark Anthony, Lancelot and Guinevere, Paris and Helen, Napoleon and Josephine, and Odysseus and Penelope. Each of these couples exhibited an overpowering love and passion for one another.

We all have a story to tell about love, an experience we cannot forget, a love deeply embedded in our hearts and minds.

Mary Jane Lopez is a fine example of a single parent who exhibits immense love for her child. This fine woman grew up in a small town named Crystal City located more than two hundred miles southwest of San Antonio, Texas. She was the second child of a small loving family. Their unity was exemplified by the fact that three generations, grandparents, parents, and children, lived together in the same house. Mary Jane married and later became pregnant. She stated, "During my second month of pregnancy, I had several issues such as bleeding, body aches and pains, massive headaches, and lack of sleep. I strongly believed the baby inside me was trying to survive. The baby was taking all my strength away. Something was wrong with my baby." Mary Jane underwent four sonograms during her pregnancy and was never told by the doctor or nurses of any issues with her child. "As far as we all knew, the child was going to be born normal. And I didn't want to know the sex of my baby before," she said.

Around a week before childbirth, Mary Jane felt anxious about the pregnancy, feeling that something just wasn't right. The baby was not moving inside her, and she feared the worst. Mary Jane noted, "My body was telling me something was wrong." As she and the baby's heart rates began spiraling downward, the doctors immediately decided to induce her.

On July 31, 1995, Mary Jane received an emergency C-section and finally gave birth to a beautiful baby girl. But she was no ordinary baby. On the contrary, she was a special child with the gift of love from God.

Mary Jane was approached by a nurse, who stated, "Did you know your baby was going to be born like that?"

She replied, "Born like what?"

The nurse immediately departed the room. Mary Jane feared the worst. "I believed my baby was dead [stillborn]."

Her pediatrician later came in and said to her, "Your daughter was born with Down syndrome, a small hole in her heart, pneumonia, and other medical complications. She is not going to make it to tomorrow. You need to call all your relatives." Mary Jane and all her family members, relatives, friends, including her friends at the Catholic church she attended, began praying for her baby. She broke down in tears after she caught sight of her child, who was surrounded by shining lights in assorted colors. To her, it was a message from God. Upon seeing her baby, Mary Jane declared, "She is going to be OK. She is beneath the limelight."

The first time Mary Jane laid eyes on her child, it was love at first sight. She subsequently named her daughter Viva Selena Marie Lopez.

Because of her medical condition, Viva was immediately flown via helicopter to San Antonio Children's Hospital and taken to the ICU, where she spent around twenty-five days recuperating. Mary Jane prayed constantly for Viva's health. She prayed earnestly, "I believe in God and Jesus. Since You sent her to me, I will take loving care of her. I promise always to love her and take care of her no matter what. I know You sent me the perfect little angel."

Viva was also christened by the nurses as a diva. One of them considered Viva to be a diva superstar. They were surprised she had been born with perfect long fingernails. Mary Jane believed it was part of having Down syndrome. Everyone at the hospital also became aware that Viva's little hands had the marks of Christ on the cross, namely, two dried bloodstains on each of her wrists and each of her palms. Viva was a unique and special child.

Unbeknownst to Mary Jane, the doctor in San Antonio who treated Viva had some of the physical characteristics of a person with Down syndrome.

"I swear that God was present, working through Viva," Mary Jane said.

Throughout her early childhood, Viva beat all the odds. Doctors predicated she would not ever be able to eat by herself, walk by herself, talk, or dress herself. They also indicated she would always need a caretaker. But Viva triumphantly beat those seemingly insurmountable odds by way of her relentless determination and love. Mary Jane provided the pure motherly motivation and unconditional love, and God provided the grace.

As a child and later as a young adult, Viva became involved in Special Olympics and the cheer squad in middle school and high school. During those years growing up, Viva was the unfortunate victim of bullying and mocking by fellow students. They belittled her because of her physical features as a person with Down syndrome. Viva would come home dejected and crying. Mary Jane, as a caring mother, would console her and demonstrate her tremendous love with hugs, kisses, and positive encouragement.

There were occasions when Viva experienced cyberbullying by individuals over the internet and on Facebook. According to Mary Jane, these people wrote horrific messages to Viva, including, "You are a bitch and a fat pig. No one wants to see you eat." They made other crude remarks such as, "You are ugly, you dress poorly, and you should not have been born." One person made a particularly rude and evil comment: "You should commit suicide."

Mary Jane was devastated and stressed out by these comments and feared for Viva's safety. Mary Jane subsequently suffered a stroke and was hospitalized for a week. She currently takes medication for her heart condition.

Mary Jane made it a point to provide Viva with excellent advice. She uttered, "If people stare at you or look hard at you, just be nice and give them a smile and say hi."

Mary Jane recalls different people approaching her and commenting, "Your daughter is sick [está malita]."

Mary Jane would politely reply, "She is not sick. She has Down syndrome. You should look it up and learn what it means."

Many people still refer to individuals with Down syndrome as sick. When I was a child, I heard people referring to people with Down syndrome as mongoloid or mentally retarded. They would ignore these special people and stay away from them.

Individuals with Down syndrome were also labeled as idiots, morons, and imbeciles. Today, these labels are considered politically incorrect, dehumanizing, and exceptionally hurtful. Now those who have Down syndrome are correctly referred to as people who are intellectually challenged. I consider them to be special, unique, and a wonderful gift from God.

Mary Jane remembers a rude and disappointing remark made by one of her best friends: "It is so sad you have to live with Viva and put up with her the rest of your life." She took this as a personal insult and ended this close friendship, which she has no regrets about.

Mary Jane commented, "My daughter is one of the most important people in my life, including my sons. I will do everything I can to protect Viva. I love her."

In years past, I had the pleasure of coaching Viva as

a participant in Champions League Sports, which is part of the Capable Kids Foundation, a nonprofit organization that provides a tremendous amount of support to the special needs community and enables children and young adults with different disabilities to be part of something important in their lives and make friendships along the way. My wife, Esmeralda, at one point served as the executive director and made it her priority to expand the organization.

The time I spent with Viva and other individuals with special needs put a big smile on my face and made me appreciate how blessed I am in life. These individuals are special in many ways than one. Each one demonstrates their own skills and talents.

I discovered that Viva stood out among them because of her outgoing, caring, loving, and friendly personality. On several occasions, I watched her voluntarily consoling other participants when they were sad or crying. She spoke mildly and provided them with comfort and encouragement.

I can unequivocally say this: Viva is an incredibly sensitive and loving person who exhibits compassion and love toward others. She is a young adult with a loving heart.

I have personally experienced Viva's underlying compassion and love. In April 2019, after I underwent surgery for appendiceal cancer, Viva called several times while I was in the hospital and after I was discharged and at home. She would be in tears, saying, "I am praying for you, Coach. I love you. Come home now. I miss you."

Mary Jane mentioned that after these telephone conversations, Viva would continue crying and praying to God for my safe recovery. During May 2019, Viva participated in the fifty-yard dash at the Special Olympics held in Weslaco, Texas. Prior to this event, she prayed to God, made the sign of the cross, and declared, "This is for Coach Al." Her heartfelt love propelled her to run fast and earn a medal, which she dedicated to me. Afterward, Viva proudly stood up at the winner's podium and with a big smile received her medal with tears in her eyes. She kissed the medal and then glanced up to the sky, saying, "Thank You, God."

I had the good fortune to speak with Viva over the phone during the coronavirus lockdowns. I asked her what she thought about love, and she exclaimed, "Love is being with my mother and my family and my friends. God and Jesus say to love everyone."

She went on to say, "I pray to God every day. I pray when I wake up in the morning and at night before going to sleep. I always say, 'Thank You, Jesus, for this new day,' and, 'Thank You, Jesus, for the healthy food. I still pray for all my family members and friends, including you, Coach Al."

"Coach Al, be happy and not afraid. I love you."

Her prayers brought chills to my body and tears to my eyes. Those loving comments brought a smile to my face and made a positive impact on my spirit. What an unforgettable experience, the utmost expression of pure love for another person.

Viva is pursuing her dreams and is currently employed as a member of the Venom Hype Squad (a hip-hop dance squad), which is part of the Rio Grande Valley (RGV) Vipers basketball team in Edinburg, Texas. She looks beautiful dressed in her red and white cheerleading outfit and spends several nights a week cheering with other cheerleaders and encouraging the audience to support their home team. According to Mary Jane, "This is Viva's calling, and this is what she loves to do: perform." She is eternally grateful that Viva has been provided with the opportunity to perform before an audience.

Viva competes annually with the Special Olympics, participating in several events, and won first place in the Polar Plunge as the audience's favorite. She recently received a personal invitation from Governor Greg Abbott of the state of Texas to attend a meeting at the capitol building in Austin, Texas with various state representatives.

Mary Jane told me, "Viva is my world and has my total,

unconditional love. She will always be known by everyone as "Viva Diva." I consider her to be a genuine, lovable person who exhibits love to others, especially her friends, whom she hugs and tells, 'I love you.'"

When we talk about love, we are talking about a delicate subject, something that can be both beneficial and detrimental to our well-being. We all prefer to be encompassed by nothing short of compassionate love, a love that provides us with the greatest satisfaction in life, a love without end.

Over the centuries, numerous poems and stories have been written about love. Some of the writers whose works on love are most famous are William Shakespeare, Pablo Neruda, Oscar Wilde, and Mark Twain. One anonymous quote goes, "Some love lasts a lifetime. True love lasts forever."

We all face many issues each day, and they can be either good or bad, or small or large. Our decisions can affect the lives of others. We must remind our spouses, sweethearts, lovers, family members, and dear friends how important they are to us. Just say these key words: "I love you."

Being seriously ill handicaps not only the person, but also the person's entire way of life. Many people are unfortunately faced with a situation of illness, something they must bear for the rest of their lives. It may be that they provide care for a family member, some other loved one, or a dear friend who is ill. But their love for the person who is sick can make an everlasting impact on that person's life. This unconditional love will encourage the sick person, lift his or her spirits, and provide him or her with a positive outlook.

One of my dearest friends, Javier, a retired corporate analyst, and his wonderful wife Alicia, a retired teacher, who reside in Central Texas, are an example of loving parents. In 1985, one of their younger sons and his girlfriend had a tumultuous relationship ending with the birth of a son, Kevin, in the spring of 1986 at a local hospital. Doctors and specialists diagnosed

Kevin with cerebral palsy, a condition that drastically affected his motor skills and optic nerves, the latter of which were frail, resulting in blindness. The doctors thus concluded that Kevin had a low life expectancy.

According to Alicia, their son's girlfriend confided in him that her mother was extremely upset with her for getting pregnant. Her parents were embarrassed by the situation and isolated her from the boyfriend. Her mother also demanded she have an abortion. The girlfriend said she feared her parents and refused to have an abortion. They in return banned her from leaving their house.

On one occasion, Javier and Alicia attempted to visit their son's girlfriend but were denied access by her mother. They were upset about being turned away and left to go back home.

Months later, their son's girlfriend gave birth to the baby boy Kevin. She informed the father of the boy's birth and indicated he was going to be put up for adoption at her mother's request. She also concealed the fact that Kevin had various medical problems and a disability. Alicia told me, "As a mother and grandmother, I was concerned. I was determined to find out what was going to become of him because they wanted him to be adopted out." To her knowledge, no one knew that baby Kevin was sick or disabled prior to his birth. This was when Alicia finally recognized that her son's girlfriend had been scared during her pregnancy, not knowing what to do.

Javier and Alicia subsequently received a letter of notification from an adoption agency informing them and their son of the birth of the baby boy, Kevin. As the bearer of shocking news, the adoption agency indicated the child was disabled with microcephaly and was being put up for adoption. The letter requested that the father relinquish the rights to his son. Further, the baby was placed in a foster home under the care of an elderly woman for several months.

Javier and Alicia were fortunately provided with the

opportunity to visit Kevin and were given the option to adopt him. They were notified of his disability and medical problems. Kevin was handicapped and would require an exceptional amount of care and more than likely would be moved from foster home to foster home, with the high likelihood of never being adopted. The adoption agency indicated Kevin was a rare case and that it was highly unlikely anyone would adopt him. Alicia declared, "Kevin never would have stood a chance in life if he had been placed in a foster home. He would not have reached adulthood or even eighteen years of age."

Initially, Javier and Alicia were deeply moved and concerned about the child and his care. They prayed earnestly to God for an answer. Soon they decided to take it upon themselves to raise their grandson Kevin as their own son, asserting themselves into his life as loving and caring parents. Alicia commented, "I had a good feeling I could care for him. I felt an overwhelming amount of love for him. I did not want to give up on him. No matter what issues he had, it did not faze me. I wanted to take care of him."

Who else could provide better care than the child's grandparents? Yes! Grandparents are known to spoil their grandkids. But this case was special; it required sacrifice, patience, care, and most notably, love—an eternal love bonding them for life!

Javier and Alicia were the perfect grandparents in caring for Kevin. They made it their priority in life to provide him with proper parenting and unconditional love.

Javier and Alicia mentioned that Kevin had been diagnosed with microcephaly and cerebral palsy, that he was legally blind, and that he had no motor skills and was confined to bed. He was unable to sit up and perform normal tasks such as walking or talking. The couple spoon-fed Kevin, bathed him, and provided him with the prescribed medications for seizures and muscle relaxants to to loosen his stiffness. Later, as Kevin grew in age, he was unable to eat and was fitted with a feeding tube and also given breathing treatments via a nebulizer.

Javier and Alicia made it their priority in life to care for Kevin. They made sure he was taken to the right doctors and specialists and that they provided him with the proper medical care.

Javier recalled a physician who defined microcephaly as a rare neurological condition or birth defect in which an infant's head is smaller than that of other children the same age. This neurological condition results in abnormal brain development. It can cause grave complications such as poor coordination, intellectual disabilities, delayed development, and seizures, among other things. The child would not function like other children or live a normal lifestyle.

Kevin was facing tremendous odds in terms of survival given his diagnoses of microcephaly and cerebral palsy. According to Javier and Alicia, the physicians gave him a slim chance of survival and said he would live only to the age of five. The odds were heavily stacked against Kevin. It would take their total commitment and sacrifice to care for him and love him.

When Kevin reached the age of five, Alicia and Javier took him to a spine specialist for his cerebral palsy. After examining Kevin, the physician made a startling and inhumane remark: "If I had a child like him, I would euthanize him because he is suffering." Also, he rudely said, "I can't help you!" According to Alicia, the physician got up and walked out, leaving her and Javier alone, staring at each other in awe, shell shocked and amazed at his response. No compassion whatsoever.

Alicia was agitated and deeply disturbed by the physician's remarks. She commented, "All this time we were trying to get help for the child. But the doctor gave us an entirely different answer instead of helping us out. I was upset as I listened to his comments. Those cruel words sank deep into my heart.

There was no way I was going to give up on Kevin. I was more determined than ever to help him."

Later that same day, the couple made the decision never to take Kevin to visit that doctor again. There was no procedure to fix his spine problem because of his spina bifida.

As Kevin grew older, Javier and Alicia continued caring for him with occupational therapy and prescription medications. Unfortunately, Kevin was unable to see or speak. To keep him comfortable in bed, they would turn on the radio for music or the television, which brought a joyful smile to Kevin's face. "He was a good baby who was content and never cried. Family members would enter his room and say, 'Hi, Kevin!' In return, he would display a big smile."

Alicia kept him comfortable and happy by reading children's storybooks to him, causing him to smile in amusement. She also sang the alphabet song and other lullabies, along with playing songs on the radio and putting cartoons on the television, which made a positive impact on Kevin.

As Kevin grew into his teen years, he showed a bit of physical development. Alicia noted, "I would care for him most of the time. A home health-care nurse also provided care during the day from eight in the morning to six at night, at least for five days of the week. As Kevin got older, he required additional help during the weekends."

Alicia told me, "I always prayed for him. When he was young, we took him to church service. We put our faith in God. We were optimistic Kevin would get better. Although his health never improved, we loved him dearly and never gave up on him."

At one point Javier and Alicia moved to a subdivision located on the outskirts of Rolla, Missouri. They took Kevin with them and resided there for nine years. They continued caring for him and at times drove more than one hundred miles for doctor's appointments. They did not take him out much because of the colder climate. After some time, they relocated to South Texas, where Kevin was more comfortable. It was a team effort among the entire family to keep Kevin comfortable and happy.

Alicia declared, "I never questioned God. I believed in Him. I prayed to God and constantly requested He heal Kevin."

When Kevin reached age twenty-four, he became severely sick with breathing issues and kidney failure. He was in constant pain; his health was deteriorating rapidly; and he required oxygen support. Alicia mentioned, "We were reluctant to place him in hospice care, but we had no other option. He was acidy and in poor health."

Alicia recalls an emotional incident at the hospital when Kevin stopped breathing and was miraculously revived by the medical staff. She was dejected and heartbroken. Javier knew he was deathly ill and was on his deathbed. During this stressful time, the couple made the painful decision to place Kevin in hospice care.

Javier and Alicia observed Kevin lying in his bed with tears in his eyes as he was suffering and in constant pain. Alicia wept for him. She was grief-stricken, exhibiting a mother's infinite love for her dying child. Little did they know this would be the last time they would look upon Kevin alive. The next day, he died peacefully.

Alicia expressed her grief: "We were heartbroken and devastated. There are no words to describe the loss of a loved one and my sadness for my grandson who became our son. We were devastated by Kevin's death. I remember the doctors initially claimed he would only live to the age of five, but with all our love and care, he lived until the age of twenty-four. Today, I am still deeply affected by the loss of Kevin."

Days later, Alicia asked her priest, "What am I going to do without him? I gave up my career to care for him."

The priest replied, "Pray for Kevin and trust in God. He is now in God's hands."

Alicia cried out, "I always had faith in God, and if something was His will, I accepted it. I left Kevin in God's hands. In the end, I accepted God's will. He has a plan for everyone."

I asked Alicia if she had any recommendations to make to families with disabled children or adults. She joyfully replied, "The first thing I would recommend is to commit all your love to the person and then have total faith. Provide for your disabled family member and take care of them the best you can. Give them all your love, and keep the faith!" Becoming emotional, she added, "I still cry for Kevin and pray for him. I miss him a great deal. I kept certain pictures, articles of clothing, and other items that belonged to him as a remembrance. I know he is in heaven and is not suffering anymore."

Javier was also emotional, saying, "At times it was difficult to care for Kevin, but thank God we were all able to provide for him. Our unconditional love made him live longer, mostly because of God's good grace and blessings." Both Javier and Alicia cried as we concluded the interview.

What a remarkable story of loving grandparents who took it upon themselves to sacrifice their careers and way of life to provide for their grandson who became their adopted son—an amazing exhibition of unconditional love for another human being! It is rare to find this type of deep-rooted love in our society, the epitome of true love!

I leave you with this final note: When everything appears to be falling apart around you and it seems your life is ending, and you believe in your heart that no one is there for you, reach out to Almighty God. He will always be there to care for you. His is a divine love beyond reproach.

Furthermore, God loves you as you, like all of us, are His child. The Bible declares, "Love never fails (it never fades or ends)" (1 Corinthians 13:8 AMP).

CHAPTER 4

GOD'S CHILDREN

For ye are all children of God by faith in Christ Jesus.

—Galatians 3:26

Children are one of life's most precious gifts. They have an innocence that is beyond reproach and pure hearts and trustingness unpolluted by others. Our beloved children are our heritage and our future. They will follow their own paths in life, carrying the torch.

But this cruel and cold world of ours changes their hearts over time. They begin to see and experience what living in this world is all about, including the corruption and immorality that exists among people and the goodness and the wickedness they will face from both atheists and believers in God. Whether or not to have faith in God is a decision they will make on their own, pursuing whether what is good or what is evil.

Many children are blessed to be born in perfect health with no issues whatsoever and grow up to live normal, healthy lives. But some children are less fortunate as they are born with different diseases or disabilities such as Down syndrome, cerebral palsy, autism (Asperger's syndrome), blindness, muscular dystrophy, dyslexia, and epilepsy, among others. These disabilities drastically affect their lives, causing them lifelong challenges. These children are at times less thought of, are considered outcasts, and are forgotten by society.

History has proven this to be true. In July 1933, the Nazi government of Germany instituted the Law for the Prevention of Progeny with Hereditary Diseases. This inhumane law called for the sterilization of all persons who suffered from diseases considered hereditary, including mental illnesses, learning disabilities, physical deformities, epilepsy, blindness, deafness, and severe alcoholism. The Third Reich utilized this law to their advantage and stepped up the propaganda against innocent people with disabilities. They regularly labeled them "life unworthy of life" or "useless eaters" and highlighted the burden they placed on society.[1]

In 1939, Adolf Hitler increased the senseless persecution of persons with disabilities by secretly authorizing a program of "mercy killing" administered by the medical profession and code-named Operation T4. This savage program led to the brutal killing of thousands of disabled Austrian and German people who were considered inferior. Some of these mass killings were conducted using poison gas. By the end of World War II, the Nazis had murdered hundreds of thousands of people with various disabilities, having considered them to be a threat to the nation's health. The Nazis also made it a priority to exclude Jews and minorities from everyday life, thus resulting in the persecution of millions of innocent people or extermination using the method known as the "Final Solution," an indescribable evil inflicted on humanity![2]

Currently, our society still assigns stigma and stereotypes to disabled persons. It will take time to educate society as a whole and change the language used to describe or talk to disabled individuals and thereby eliminate the stigma.

In today's world, it takes special parents who are caring and loving to raise a child or young adult with disabilities, parents who understand the child's issues, who are patient and understanding, and who show the child unconditional love. It is a great sacrifice that such people make for the sake of their loved ones.

An article I read recently on a website called *Raising the Extraordinary* from October 8, 2018, on the topic of special needs, raises questions and concerns on behalf of a churchgoing mother. It is titled "Dear Church, Children with Special Needs Are God's Children Too."[3]

This mother and her husband have a daughter with special needs, and they were attending service at a church where they had been members for many years. Their daughter was in a separate room participating in the children's ministry and was subsequently removed from that room and taken to another location. According to the mother, by excluding the child from the service, it sent a message to the other children and parishioners indicating it is OK to cast these individuals out.

At the end she writes, "Special needs or not, our children are just that, children. They are God's child just like all the other children. They still need Jesus, still need to be loved, still need to know that they are an indispensable part of the body of Christ."[4]

I highly commend this woman for standing up for the rights of her child and making the church aware that it is not OK to exclude a person who has any type of disability. Instead, the church should make the proper accommodations and educate its employees and parishioners in how to properly serve these individuals. Other businesses should also make the proper accommodations.

This raises an especially poignant question: who are God's children?

The Bible indicates that God offers us the opportunity to be His children. In 1 John 3:1, we read, "See what great the love the Father has lavished on us, that we should be called children of God" (NIV). And John 1:12–13 tells us, "To all who received

Him, to those who believed in His name, He gave the right to become children of God ... children born ... but born of God" (NIV).

As mentioned earlier, God considers all of us to be His children. He does not differentiate between healthy people and those stricken with a disability or disease. God considers us all the same. Remember that He created us in His own image. This is noted in Genesis 1:27: "So God created mankind in his own image, in the image of God he created them; male and female he created them" (NIV).

During one of our organization's monthly group sessions, a concerned parent stood up and voiced her concerns about raising a disabled child. She mentioned how she and her husband had fervently prayed to God to give them a healthy child. They were later blessed with a baby girl. Unfortunately, she had a disability, namely, Down syndrome. They believed that God had punished them for their mistrust in Him. A psychologist, who was the featured speaker, replied, "We do not know God's plan for everyone. But He miraculously replaced one joy with another joy you were not expecting. You and all of us should always be thankful and rejoice in a gift provided by God. No matter if the child is healthy or has a disability, they are God's child too."

God has a plan and a purpose for everyone, including children and adults with disabilities. He gracefully performs things (i.e., miracles) that they cannot discern. But when sickness or disability happens to us, unfortunately, we either question God or doubt Him. We need to put more trust and faith in God.

Many parents struggle each day to raise their child or children (or young adult[s]) with special needs. It is not an easy task. It can become burdensome, stressful, and painful and can also take a heavy toll on their own lives and the lives of their loved ones.

Do such people blame God and question Him, asking, "Why

me? Is it my fault? Is God punishing me for something I did or did not do? Have my sins in life finally caught up to me?"

No! Of course not! God has a definite plan and an important reason for everything and everyone in existence.

We must stay positive and continuously trust in God. We must thank Him daily and glorify Him.

It is through God's grace and power that we are blessed with a special needs child. There is a definite reason and a plan for the child's life and for our own, a plan set by God, a plan that we as humans do not comprehend! This is one of life's greatest mysteries.

A close relative, Alex, age nineteen, is a testament to all I've just said. He was diagnosed by medical professionals with Asperger's syndrome (a "high-functioning" type of autism) at the age of six.

Initially, it was difficult for his mother, Victoria, and his father, Bob, to accept the results and believe he had any type of disability. They were not fully aware of this medical condition and did not know how to respond. Several of their family members would comment that Alex was a spoiled child. These people were also unaware of his condition.

Bob said, "I questioned God on several occasions: Why us? Why him, my son? How are we going to raise him? What do we do? How are we going to do this? What resources are available out there to assist him?" These and many more questions cluttered his mind.

Bob and Victoria realized God had provided them with a special gift, that is, a child with an amazing mind, a child they cared for, adored, and loved with all their hearts. They saw him as a normal child who had been blessed by God with a special gift (i.e., his mind).

As an Aspie, Alex had trouble socializing with others and preferred to be alone. He exhibited anxiety, nervousness, and clumsiness, at times with repetitive motions and weird behavior.

To combat this behavior, his parents organized a routine for him. According to Victoria, Alex was also unable to empathize when other children were crying or hurt. he would ask his parents, "Why are they crying? There is no reason to cry! There is nothing wrong." Alex was narrow-minded and focused on certain objects or toys. He loved to play with the different dinosaurs and knew the names of all the Thomas the Train toys. He would line up the toys in order and name them all.

Alex had a brilliant mind and remembered details of events and historical dates. Bob and Victoria were astonished with him. But to him, the world was black and white with no gray areas. Things were either right or wrong, either true or false. There was no middle ground. He would not budge.

Many times when in elementary and middle school, Alex complained he had been victimized by bullies. They would make fun of his character and push him around. Alex confided in Victoria, "They were rude and made fun of me because of my social character and physical stature. They were also not on par with my intelligence." Alex refused to provide his mother with any further information, primarily because of the bad memories resurfacing and haunting him. He did not want to recall these horrific experiences. They were better locked away in a closet, a dark place he refused to explore and therefore forgot.

Victoria recalled an incident in elementary school when she and Bob were called to the principal's office. A history teacher had made the absurd complaint that their son had corrected something she said about World War II. The teacher mistakenly declared World War II had started in 1941. She was not specific as to where the war began or what country started it. Alex in return corrected her in front of the class and indicated World War II began in 1939. The teacher was embarrassed and outraged with his remarks, referring to him as being overly rude and providing him with a stern warning.

Victoria indicated Alex was devastated and confused. In his

mind, he was correct about the historic date. But his delivery was too direct and socially inappropriate. He still needed to sharpen his social skills as an Aspie.

Victoria and Bob were irate with the principal and teacher because of Alex's scolding. During their conversation, they informed them of Alex's sensitive condition being an Aspie. Their response was cold with no empathy. Victoria and Bob's son had embarrassed the teacher. The principal wanted Alex to apologize to his teacher for being disrespectful and rude in front of the class. This was more important to them than Alex's condition.

Alex again complained to Victoria and Bob saying that several students constantly bullied him, one of whom was in his class. This student allegedly made verbal and written threats via computer messages to other students. To settle the matter, Victoria took the initiative. She set up an appointment with the school principal to discuss these issues in detail. When Victoria and Bob mentioned the potential threat to Alex, the principal and teacher shook their heads in disbelief. Their reply was a defensive no. They did not believe such a thing was occurring in their school. To Victoria and Bob's disbelief, the school protected the aggressors and not the innocent victim, their son. The principal's recommendation was to remove Alex from the classroom and insert him into another class, saying this would fix the problem. This made Victoria even more irate. She commented, "Of course, punish the victim and not the aggressor. An effortless way out of the situation."

Victoria and Bob replied sternly and inquired why the school was choosing not to remove the potentially dangerous student who was the actual bully allegedly making the threats. The principal was cold and would not budge. Victoria said, "It was disheartening to listen to their reply and recognize how incompetent and unknowledgeable they were concerning children with disabilities. Also, they made no acknowledgment of the bullying occurring in their own school right under their noses."

Victoria and Bob left the meeting flabbergasted and shaking their heads in disbelief. They took Alex home. He was dejected and was crying for having been mistreated and misunderstood. It took them several hours of consoling to calm him down. Victoria said, "This is a textbook example of how children with disabilities such as autism are misunderstood and treated differently in school and society. The schools' priorities are not in line with the handling of special needs children."

Several days later, Victoria and Bob made the right decision to remove Alex from that school and to homeschool him instead. This was a blessing for him. He sobbed and commented that he was free at last from the bullies. He was now able to enjoy life and concentrate on his studies.

Victoria and Bob made it a priority to research Asperger's syndrome to educate themselves and provide Alex with the tools and the love he needed to succeed in life. They became aware of their need to change their lifestyle to better accommodate Alex. Bob said, "As parents, we must fully understand we have a commitment to our children. It is our duty and responsibility, and no one else's, to educate them in moral values and teach them how to survive without us in a changing society. We must provide them with a positive avenue to succeed in life. Also, we must change to provide these children with a better quality of life. It is not them who explicitly need to change. It is us! This was hard to accept initially, but when reality of the situation hit us square in the face, it was then that we started to fully trust in our faith and in God. There was nowhere else to turn."

I highly recommend the unique and informative book written by Tony Attwood titled *The Complete Guide to Asperger's Syndrome* (2007), a tremendous resource for parents and professionals that provides a wealth of information on all aspects of the syndrome from childhood to adulthood. It lists the definition of Asperger's syndrome and talks about social conditioning, friendships, bullying, and theories about the mind, expression, and emotions of Aspies, also exploring their special interests, cognitive behavior, and language and providing other valuable information.[5]

I have read parts of this book, and it has helped me to better understand children with autism, including the reasons why they behave in certain ways, their thought process and sensory perception, and how others and the environment can affect them in a positive or negative way. This book is of great benefit and serves as a guide for parents who are dealing with an Aspie. There are other books I recommend that parents purchase to help them to know, raise, and understand their child. We must remind ourselves to educate others and all members of society so they will better understand people with autism.

Several years ago, my wife and I had the opportunity to meet numerous families with children and young adults stricken with various disabilities. It was through our nonprofit organization—501 (c)(3)—named Aware RGV, and a similar organization named the Capable Kids Foundation, that were truly able to participate in different events such as monthly support groups, adaptive sports, fundraisers, and a special needs conference. During these extraordinary events, we socialized with many parents and their children or young adults who were enthusiastic to participate and be accepted by others.

My wife used the motto "Awareness and Acceptance" specifically to benefit those individuals with a disability who were underrepresented and underserved. She voiced her concern that the local government and the community were not taking the proper steps to provide the essential resources to accommodate these individuals and allow them to live up to their God-given potential. She declared, "They are God's children just like each and every one of us. They also need a voice and benefits like everyone else. Nothing sets them apart from us. Further, they are living and breathing human beings who have the same emotions and feeling that we do."

My wife and I became friends with countless parents and their children. Special relationships were established, and we all became part of an extraordinary, unique, close-knit family of people who understand each other's dilemmas, issues, and concerns and are willing to help each other in times of need.

My wife had been introduced to Maritza Ramirez previously during a fundraising event as a potential sponsor of the Capable Kids Foundation. Maritza is the chief operating officer and managing partner of a document shredding and storage company and also the owner/partner of another business. She is a single mom and has three lovely children. The family resides in Mission, Texas.

I contacted Maritza and inquired about her involvement in supporting children and adults with cancer. Maritza replied, "My grandpa died from colon cancer. Also, one of our high school classmates named Eduardo 'Eddie' Vela was diagnosed with terminal cancer. It hit us hard because we were young. Thus, I made the decision to get involved in helping people with cancer."

In 1996, Eddie graduated from Mission High School and pursued a career in law enforcement as a United States Border Patrol (USBP) agent. Maritza, her sister, and some friends, including Eddie, were all close and hung out together.

When Eddie became a USBP agent, he worked in the Rio Grande Valley sector of South Texas. Several years later, he became ill and was immediately hospitalized with appendicitis. Unfortunately, he was diagnosed with appendiceal cancer and was released from the hospital.

Eddie underwent cancer treatments at a hospital in McAllen and subsequently underwent treatments at MD Anderson Hospital in Houston. After several surgeries and chemotherapy treatments, he seemed at times to be better. Maritza and other friends organized fundraisers to raise funds for the family's travel expenses.

During this period of hardship, Eddie and his wife, Brandy, had a newborn son and she was out of work. This dilemma placed them in a financial bind. Maritza spearheaded the fundraising events and said that Eddie too was faithful to the cause.

Prior to his death, Eddie and Maritza held a significant conversation about who would continue as head of his own foundation. Eddie commented, "I want to help other people like you helped me. Let's start a foundation and raise money for people." Maritza was excited and agreed to help him out.

Eddie started the foundation without the knowledge he was not going to survive his battle with cancer. He said, "If I die, make sure our foundation helps my fellow agents."

His main effort was to help other agents in the Rio Grande Valley and provide them with financial assistance. Eddie's final decision was a blessing to Maritza. In case of his death, she would assume the leadership role for the foundation.

After a valiant two-year battle with cancer, in 2008 Eduardo "Eddie" Vela succumbed to the disease at the age of thirty-two. He left behind his loving wife, Brandy, and their one-year-old son, Jordan.

Eddie had a saying: "All I need is faith, family, and friends." He used this phrase on his Facebook page, and later it was stamped into rubber bracelets. Eventually it became the name of the foundation, which was founded in 2009 as the Faith, Family, & Friends Foundation—Eddie and Brandy Vela's vision to raise funds and help others who are battling cancer. The foundation's primary goal and mission is to assist federal agents and their family members in their struggle with cancer.

As the head of the foundation, Maritza's goal was to raise enough funds to help support families who were fighting cancer. Each year, she would hold several fundraising events, such as a golf tournament, raffles, and car washes, to raise the much-needed funds to benefit others.

I personally received some of the benefits offered by this foundation. In January 2019, I was hospitalized at Methodist Hospital in San Antonio, Texas, with appendiceal cancer such as Mr. Eddie Vela had experienced. Maritza contacted my wife and offered financial support from this outstanding foundation. I was a government employee, and during this time of federal government shutdown, employees were furloughed and did not receive paychecks. At this point, I had missed three paychecks, and Esmeralda and I were financially burdened, unable to pay bills such as our mortgage. Maritza was gracious enough to provide us with the necessary funds to cover part of our mortgage payment. Her generosity was of tremendous benefit to my family in this time of urgent need.

I was speechless, emotional, and teary-eyed, thanking God for their gracious generosity. My sincere thanks to Maritza and Brandy Vela, and especially to Mr. Eddie Vela, a fellow federal law enforcement agent, whose heart of gold and golden spirit helped and comforted many families including mine. Their amazing overture tremendously impacted my life, and I am forever thankful and grateful. Eddie's legacy lives on today! (*Note:* I took a short break from writing the rest of the story because of its emotional impact on me.)

Every day I thank God for all His many blessings! His eternal grace has prolonged my life. Furthermore, God gave me a golden opportunity to spend more quality time on earth with my family and friends. I have the phrase "Trust in God" forever etched in my heart and mind.

Maritza continued her volunteer work and decided to take some of the funds to start another organization to help society. This new organization, named the Greater Gold Foundation, was founded as a resource for families facing a diagnosis of childhood cancer. On any given day, more than one thousand children are battling cancer in the Rio Grande Valley area of South Texas. Maritza and her associates participate in raising funds and continue to be a valuable resource for these families. All funds raised are used to financially support the foundation and the children of the Vannie E. Cook Children's Cancer and Hematology Clinic, which is very important as this is the only cancer clinic for children in the RGV. Greater Good also makes it a priority to raise awareness and find a cure for childhood cancer. This cancer, just like the others we are aware of, does not discriminate.

Maritza's foundations also provide support to families with other types of disabilities.

Maritza exclaimed, "I found my purpose in life, which is to help others on earth, especially those battling cancer."

Maritza shared four profound stories of children battling cancer. The first was of a young boy named Jesus, whose cancer was terminal. In 2015, the foundation received an application from a woman in Donna, Texas, seeking assistance paying for her young son's funeral. Maritza contacted the woman, Amanda, who was desperate and needed help. Her son had not died yet, but she was told he was going to die soon. Amanda lived in a poor neighborhood and had no funds to assist her terminally ill son. Jesus was battling cancer and previously had an arm surgically removed because of the cancer. Maritza met with them both and offered the foundation's services.

Jesus loved football, especially his hometown football team, the Donna Redskins. Maritza made it a priority to contact the head football coach and tell him of Jesus's diagnosis with terminal cancer and his love for football. They set up a meeting and agreed to accommodate Jesus.

During October, Jesus participated in a Donna, Texas, homecoming parade and also went out on the field at halftime during the homecoming football game. Several football players carried him on their shoulders onto the field like a true hero.

Unfortunately, Jesus's health began to deteriorate, and several months later, in December, he died. Dejected and emotional, members of the Donna Redskins football team served as pallbearers at the church and the cemetery.

This dreadful incident affected Maritza and gave her the courage and motivation to pursue fundraising for children with cancer. She inquired into the Vannie Cook Clinic in McAllen, asking what assistance they provided and what research into childhood cancer they had conducted.

Maritza declared, "I know a lot of adults battling cancer, but a child battling cancer is life-changing. They are God's children and need more exceptional care and treatment."

Maritza further expressed, "Children are strong and do not complain. They are not aware of what is happening to their bodies. They are more resilient than adults many times."

After the incident with Jesus, Maritza made a commitment to educate herself about childhood cancer and research the topic to help others in need. She made it her life's mission to spread the word throughout the RGV about childhood cancer.

She told me, "Kids are dying, and no one is paying attention. We need to do more for these kids. It changed my life and made an impact on me as a mother once I noticed that other people are suffering in this world."

Maritza's main desire is to spread awareness in the Rio Grande Valley by visiting each school district and meeting directly with superintendents, board members, principals, teachers, and whomever else will listen to her. She has accomplished much toward her effort and task in the past two years, having convinced most RGV school districts to participate in an event commemorating childhood cancer.

Many schools and the community at large participate in Breast Cancer Awareness Month each October. This is always a big event all throughout the RGV. Maritza stressed, "September is Childhood Cancer Awareness Month, but no one was recognizing these kids with cancer."

According to Maritza, it was very important for the local school districts to participate in this event. She got in touch with the various schools and convinced them to be part of Childhood Cancer Awareness Month. They were only recognizing breast cancer in October, when they filled up the local football stadiums with participants all dressed in pink. But the spotlight also should have been on children battling cancer, who were not being recognized with their cause not being adequately addressed.

The organization produced a program and Maritza purchased gold-colored rubber bracelets with her own funds. She convinced football coaches and players to wear the bracelets and meet prior to the game to honor the children battling cancer. Many of the schoolteachers and students were unaware of the number of children in their district who were battling all types of cancers, with the victims ranging in age from newborn to eighteen.

Maritza stated, "I have seen newborn babies with cancer. One of the moms was healthy, and as soon as the baby was born and the umbilical cord was cut, the baby was diagnosed with cancer." The baby girl, named Landon, was diagnosed an extraordinarily aggressive form of leukemia, a blood-like cancer. This was an incredibly sad situation to have to face. But fortunately, Landon is still alive thanks to the grace of God.

Maritza noted, "We produced a program, and I used my own money to buy a bunch of gold wristbands to wear as a memento for children with cancer."

Last year alone, the foundation distributed more than ten thousand wristbands, which resemble a sweatband with a gold ribbon running through it, throughout the RGV.

Maritza's ambitious goal is to get the entire state of Texas involved in childhood cancer awareness. She specified, "If people become aware, then they will care."

Sadly, many people are not aware of childhood cancer. Many of these kids tried to attend school but had to drop out because they were battling this fatal disease. They needed to travel to get the proper treatments such as chemotherapy. Some families relocated to areas like Houston, where MD Anderson Hospital is located.

Most parents reprioritize their lives with one of them being forced to quit their job to care for the sick child and not leave the child alone. According to Maritza, people often face the alternative of selling their homes or vehicles to pay the medical expenses. Some parents fall into extreme poverty, with some being in a position of being unable to feed themselves, having made an enormous sacrifice to care for a child.

The next story is about a loving, caring mother who took a big risk in swimming across the Rio Grande River carrying her dying son in her arms. She valiantly fought the current to make it safely into the United States to provide her son Angel with the proper medical treatment. He was diagnosed with leukemia and later went into remission. Her other young son, Edwin, was soon thereafter diagnosed with cancer too. The older son, Angel, relapsed and was later diagnosed with testicular cancer. It is unbelievable that both these children, riddled with cancer, came from healthy parents with no medical problems.

Angel and Edwin both underwent treatment at the Vannie E. Cook Jr. Children's Cancer and Hematology Clinic, which discriminates against no one, even those who are in the country illegally (i.e., not US citizens). The center helped a great deal in the treatment of both brothers, who are currently alive and participating in soccer. Their parents are currently employed, making the ultimate sacrifice for their sons and better way of life in the United States.

The third story entails a young boy with lung cancer who was in Houston with his mother. Some people had made inappropriate comments about him on Facebook and made fun of him. One of their cruel comments was, "Game over for you, buddy. You are going to die."

Maritza was totally upset with these bullying types of comments. She exclaimed, "I was appalled and irate with people in our society who are cruel and evil with no remorse and no compassion for others, especially when they target and belittle an innocent child who is fighting for his life."

Maritza began a program of partnering up several kids with cancer and introducing them to student athletes. Athletes are sometimes school role models, admired by their fellow students. This program has enabled the athletes to appreciate life more and to be grateful for the gift that God has graced them with.

Several of these children with cancer delivered emotional speeches about their life-changing experience in front of student athletes from different schools. They detailed their daily sufferings and their struggle to survive. They also described how cancer had totally changed their lives and hindered them from participating in any sports. This program provided an eye-opening experience and encouragement to the athletes and the other students.

Although many people live their lives without caring about others, Maritza has made it her goal to find those individuals who do care and want to have a positive influence on others' lives. It should be noted that Maritza's middle child, a daughter, is intellectually challenged with a low IQ and has been victimized by bullies at school.

Maritza further voiced, "Some people live their whole lives not knowing their life's purpose. Others do not care and do not open their eyes to God. Sometimes God opens their eyes to help them recognize and help others. I am exceedingly grateful that God put my life's purpose in front of me: to help others and to help kids with cancer and their families. God gave me the heart for this work. He also gave me the ability for it."

Maritza recalled her church pastor giving a beautiful sermon on the beatitudes, in which we learn that God blesses us so that we may be a blessing to others. She said, "I am blessed more than I ever imagined I would be. And I am blessed to be a blessing."

The scripture makes it clear that God blesses us and that we can bless others and give cheerfully. He has given each of us different talents that we can utilize for the benefit of others. Hebrews 13:16 tells us, "And do not forget to do good and to share with others, for with such sacrifices God is pleased" (NIV).

I asked Maritza if she had any recommendations for families who have children with cancer or other disabilities. She replied cheerfully, "If you are going through hardships, reach out to other people. Never lose faith, and never give up."

The fourth and final story pertains to a beautiful and lovable young girl named Kaitlyn who was diagnosed with cancer and had been struggling with it for several years. She underwent numerous chemotherapy treatments to prolong her life. But in the end, God had a different plan for her.

Maritza told me the brief version of her experience with Kaitlyn and her mother, Roxanne. Approximately four years ago, Maritza received a call at five in the morning from Roxanne, who quietly inquired what she was doing. Maritza was asleep at the time and asked how Kaitlyn was doing. Roxanne replied that Kaitlyn was fine and had requested to talk to Maritza.

This baffled Maritza. She declared, "I had just met with her the day before, and she was in immense pain, couldn't speak, and couldn't move. I knew her days were few." Kaitlyn then came onto the phone and said in a sweet and tender voice, "Hi, Maritza."

Maritza was in total shock and could not believe what she was hearing. Kaitlyn invited her over. Maritza agreed and rushed over to meet with Kaitlyn and her mom.

Prior to this special moment, Maritza had been praying intensely for months for God to perform a miracle and heal Kaitlyn. Several weeks later, Maritza spoke with a pastor concerning Kaitlyn's grave condition. The pastor suggested that the congregation pray for mercy on Kaitlyn's behalf. This would enable her frail body to rest and would soothe her pain and suffering.

When Maritza arrived, Kaitlyn was sitting in bed. Maritza was mesmerized by her presence. For the past several months, she had not seen Kaitlyn sit up without it causing her pain. Staring right at Kaitlyn, she could not believe her eyes.

Roxane was exhausted and left for the other room to get some much-needed rest. Maritza and Kaitlyn were alone for a few hours. They cherished the quality time, talking, laughing, and praying. In those precious moments, Maritza observed a different Kaitlyn. She told me, "I am forever grateful I saw Kaitlyn healed for a few hours. I witnessed a little girl whom I loved given mercy!"

Maritza never understood why Kaitlyn suffered tremendously. As they held hands for the final time, Kaitlyn said a little prayer and uttered, "I love You, Jesus."

As Maritza departed the residence, she knew she would never see Kaitlyn alive again. God had given her this special time with her to say goodbye and to witness her in a healed condition, if only for a short while. It was a special gift provided from above.

Kaitlyn was faithful until the end. Several hours later, she succumbed to cancer. Maritza proclaimed, "Not a day goes by that she does not cross my mind. For Kaitlyn, to know her was to love her. And to love her was a blessing. Kaitlyn will forever be missed by her family and friends. She was a child of God who never lost faith."

Maritza has been a Christian all her life. But not until that special moment alone with Kaitlyn was she able to experience the peace and presence of God in the room with them. Throughout the night, Kaitlyn made comments that made an impact on Maritza's life.

Kaitlyn was an amazing, joyous, wonderful, loving, and faithful young girl who brightened the lives of many on her journey home to heaven. She will never be forgotten.

Our children, no matter if they are healthy or ill, good or bad, are our greatest gift and a blessing from God. Let us cherish each moment we have in this world with them. Let us provide our children with the proper encouragement and urge them to succeed in life. Love them and help them in any way. It is our duty and our role as parents. As Psalm 127:3–5 says, "Lo, children are a heritage of the Lord: And the fruit of the womb is his reward."

CHAPTER 5

EXPECT MIRACLES

I can do all things through Christ which strengthens me.

—Philippians 4:13

We as human beings are a unique species with an intuitive mind and the God-given gift of free will.

We tend to utilize this free will to our own advantage, at times without wondering beforehand if it will affect someone else in a negative way. If there is a successful outcome, then we will be joyous.

While some of us make the right/correct choices in life, others decide to take shortcuts and make incorrect or unlawful/illegal choices. Such choices, whether good or bad, also have either a negative or a positive outcome.

There are those among us who are easily manipulated by people who are extremely greedy—great manipulators and con artists—and who fill their pocketbooks with other people's money through fraud and theft. They utilize whatever means or methods available to them to their own advantage to amass money.

For example, in the United States, there are a number of famous televangelists who have a global outreach and bring in multiple millions of dollars each year, utilizing propaganda as their main tool to collect cash from people. They emphasize that anyone who donates is planting a seed. In return, that one small gracious seed will grow and multiply your yield. And they use scripture to back up their claims!

Several of these ministers claim to have performed miracle healings on people with different diseases or a disability, but these claims are unproven. These ministers live an extravagant lifestyle, and their primary focus is to get people to donate money to their respective churches. Their evangelical programs all follow the same format and reach the thousands and maybe millions of people all over the world who are seeking God's help.

But our primary focus in this chapter is not on miracles purported to have occurred during the ministry of one of these televangelists, or should I say modern-day faith healers. It is on the complete opposite, a real miracle—the miraculous cure of a person with cancer, some other disease, or a disability. What we might see as a miracle, another person may not.

Dictionary.com defines *miracle* as "an effect or extraordinary event in the physical world that surpasses all known human or natural powers and is ascribed to a supernatural event."[1]

Unbelievable! A supernatural event!

So, people consider a miracle to be an extraordinary event caused by the infinite power of Almighty God.

The Bible, which many of us have read, provides full descriptions of the miracles performed by Jesus Christ and several of his apostles. It also lists miracles of other famous people who trusted in God and were under the influence of the Holy Spirit, such as Moses, Elijah, Daniel, David, and Noah. These miracles were accomplished because of the faith of our Lord, of the person He cured, or of other concerned parties. These genuine miracles, witnessed by hundreds or thousands of people, were divinely inspired by the Holy Spirit to be carried out by people who were under the direct authority of God.

Many of the poor souls whom Jesus and His disciples healed had been ravaged by disease, such as leprosy; were deformed, such as with blindness; were possessed by demons; or had died. The living ones all placed their firm faith in Jesus Christ and God, which resulted in the most extraordinary gift a person could ever receive: a miracle.

A miracle! It is a miracle to be healed, to avoid death, and to be free to go on living life!

A close friend of my wife named Carla had this to say about surviving cancer: "After I was diagnosed with breast cancer, I underwent surgery and months of chemotherapy and radiation treatments. My last MRI disclosed I was completely free of cancer. I believe God performed a miracle by healing me. I genuinely believe in miracles. I give all the glory to God."

I had the privilege to meet another cancer survivor, Pamela, the mother of four children, who was also stricken with breast cancer and survived. She exclaimed, "I am a miracle. I survived cancer. Miracles are real. God is impressive! Stay strong and keep the faith!"

Other individuals have experienced a supernatural healing from a life-threatening disease or a disability. They attribute it to something supernatural outside their control. But as Christians, we understand this is a divine experience made possible by our faith in God and Jesus Christ and by the power of the Holy Spirit.

A notable example of God working a miracle is what happened to one of our Christian friends. In 2015, my wife and I met this woman, Ira Cobos, at a group meeting of families with disabled children and young adults. We struck up a friendly conversation with Ira, and our acquaintance evolved into a friendship. Ira subsequently was appointed to the board of AWARE-RGV, the nonprofit organization my wife and I founded.

Ira is a Christian woman married to Ruben Cobos, and they have two adult children, a twenty-four-year-old daughter named Kendra and a twenty-six-year-old son named Chauncy.

We subsequently met their two children, who volunteered to assist disabled children while they were participating in adaptive sporting events.

Ira is a sweet and gentle person with a kind heart for helping disabled children and young adults. One of the main reasons she is so involved is that she is very close to her son, Chauncy, who has Asperger's syndrome and dyslexia.

The other day, I had a brief phone conversation with Ira about Chauncy. She told me the following story:

At the age of seventeen, Ira had ovarian cysts, which had damaged her fallopian tubes. The ob-gyn who tried to reconstruct Ira's fallopian tubes told her some shocking news: she would never be able to conceive. Ira was heartbroken and extremely disappointed. But as time passed, she began to think of adopting a child, or even fostering one, if she were to ever marry. To her credit, she knew there were many foster kids in need of decent homes and families to give them a second chance at life. Ira was willing to take a chance and provide a foster child with a better opportunity.

In her midtwenties, Ira met Ruben. As their relationship progressed, they began to talk about getting married someday. She told Ruben the sad news that she was unable to bear children. He replied, "Who is bigger than God? What the doctor told you doesn't mean anything. God can do anything, even perform miracles. If we can't have any kids, then we'll adopt kids or foster a child, or whatever you want to do."

Ruben later proposed, and the couple eventually married in 1990. They left the matter of Ira's inability to bear children in God's hands. Ira commented, "I prayed to God and said, 'If this is Your plan and Your will, then fine. Lord, if it's Your will, it's Your will.'"

To her and Ruben's astonishment, three years later Ira became pregnant. She was extremely surprised and ecstatic about the pregnancy. Based on the doctor's previous conclusion, she would never bear a child. She was five months pregnant when she first became aware of her pregnancy. She had previously skipped her menstrual cycle for months at a time and therefore didn't think anything when in recent months she had missed her period. Then gastrointestinal issues and the resulting normal stomach size prevented her body from showing any signs of pregnancy. Ira was nauseous all the time, was vomiting, and felt sick and worn out. She was concerned she might have a serious underlying health problem—a stomach issue—and didn't give a thought to possibly being pregnant.

Ira confided in her best friend about being sick. Her friend was joyous and said, "You're pregnant!" Yes! You are pregnant!"

Ira smiled, then responded, "I suspect you are the one who is pregnant." Her friend continued to smile and kept saying that Ira was pregnant.

Ira purchased a home pregnancy test and was astonished when the result turned out to be positive. Thinking it might be a false positive, she asked Ruben to go to the local store and purchase a second home pregnancy test, but a different brand. Ruben purchased the item and hastily returned home. Ira retook the test, and both were amazed and in awe that the result was positive.

The next day, Ira visited her family doctor and underwent a sonogram and other tests, which confirmed her pregnancy. The calculation was that she'd been pregnant five months.

Ira and Ruben were both ecstatic about the amazing news, which spread like wildfire among their family members and close friends.

Ira told me, "Several months prior, Ruben had given his heart to the Lord. I had rededicated my life to the Lord. We also decided to get baptized together. It was also during this time I was pregnant with Chauncy, which is a tremendous blessing."

Ruben and Ira were living in Corpus Christi, Texas, at the time of her pregnancy. She began having contractions six months in and was given special medication to stop them. Her body was going into labor, so she feared the worst: miscarriage.

The doctors were baffled, unable to understand how she had been able to get pregnant with her previous health problems. Ira laughed it off with a cheerful smile. She declared, "My pregnancy was a miracle! A blessing from God!"

At times, Ira experienced severe contractions, and on several of these occasions she was admitted to the hospital for observation. There, she had an IV in her arm to deliver a higher dose of the same medication she was taking to stop the contractions. As her pregnancy continued, the doctors were very concerned about her health and the baby's health. To prevent further complications, they placed her on bed rest for the next few months.

One night when Ira's contractions and labor pains were happening with great frequency, she felt uneasy about the pregnancy. Ruben, deeply concerned, immediately rushed her to the local hospital. The doctors discovered Ira's contractions were drastically affecting the baby's heart, which would stop beating whenever she was having them. These life-threatening episodes drastically decreased his chances of survival. Thus, the doctors decided to perform an emergency C-section.

Ruben contacted his sisters-in-law and church members, who began a prayer group. Two prayer chains were ongoing for Ira's and the baby's well-being. Later, to Ira's surprise, she underwent a natural birth instead of the emergency C-section.

In June 1993, Chauncy was born six weeks premature and immediately was placed in an incubator. He had fluid in his lungs and was kept under observation for more than a week. After he was discharged, Ira and Ruben took him home. At the time, the child was very small, weighing five pounds and several ounces.

Ira breastfed Chauncy for several months, but he was unable to gain weight. The doctors prescribed a special powdered milk to help him gain weight. After his first birthday, Chauncy was given his mandatory immunizations. Soon thereafter, the family relocated to Mission, Texas.

At the age of five, Chauncy was placed in pre-K, when Ira became aware that he acted differently from the other children. She said, "Chauncy was different. He would play and entertain himself with trivial things such as a straw, a string, or a piece of paper. He was totally into dinosaurs and played with them and lined them up in order of length or height or by type of dinosaur. The way he did things was different from other kids. He was a loner." She added, "Chauncy was talkative and wanted to play with the other kids, but they didn't understand him or his way. They wouldn't follow his lead. Chauncy, instead, decided to play his own way, alone, and do his own thing."

Chauncy was in a private school where the other students often picked on him. The schoolteacher indicated Chauncy would not pay attention and performed differently in class. He would do his own thing. He was in his own little world, daydreaming. Ira also observed this. When Chauncy was at home watching television, she had to turn off the TV to get his attention. Again, he would be in his own dreamworld.

A trip to the local pediatrician and an examination of Chauncy disclosed no issues. The doctor advised Ira to stop creating a problem, saying that her son was responsive and fine. Ira then believed that she was just worried for no reason.

Chauncy later entered first grade at a public elementary school. At the end of the year, the teacher advised Ira they would be holding Chauncy back a year because he was unable to read. Ira was irate and asked why she hadn't been informed of this. The teacher just reiterated that Chauncy couldn't read. Ira again questioned their decision.

The teacher replied, "When Chauncy doesn't listen, I just leave him alone."

The following day, Ira went back to the school accompanied by a friend, who was a teacher, and they inquired about Chauncy's attendance. Chauncy's teacher became defensive and would not provide a definite answer. Regrettably, Chauncy was indeed held back a year.

The following year, Chauncy underwent several examinations and was diagnosed with central sensitivity syndrome, a form of dyslexia. Ira then made sure he obtained the proper therapies to assist him.

On one occasion, she visited the Barnes & Noble bookstore in McAllen with a friend. On her way out of the women's bathroom, she saw several books on the shelves nearby that caught her attention. One book in particular claimed to provide detailed insight into autism. Ira took the book off the shelf and flipped through it. To her amazement, Chauncy perfectly fit the profile of a child with autism. She was baffled and finally concluded that her son was unique and different from other children.

Ira told me, "I committed myself to researching autism and discovering how I could better help Chauncy enjoy a normal life."

Her persistence and determination eventually paid off. She broached the topic of autism to Chauncy's new schoolteacher, and the teacher agreed he undergo some tests. After undergoing several tests, Chauncy was diagnosed with dyslexia and high-functioning Asperger's.

Ira continued to gather information concerning autism and implemented various techniques to help Chauncy adapt and develop.

Chauncy later attended middle school and continued on to high school, at which time he joined the choir with various performances throughout the school year. This enabled him to talk to the other students and make friends.

After graduating from high school, Chauncy applied for a federal grant to implement Project HIRE (Helping Individuals Reach Employment) at South Texas College, McAllen, this grant was set up for students with disabilities to further their education and reach their goals.

Chauncy was awarded the grant, so he enrolled at South Texas College and pursued a career in culinary arts. After two years, he received a certificate in culinary arts and was later employed as a cook at the University of Texas–Rio Grande Valley (UTRGV).

Ira was pleased that Chauncy was becoming more independent and more of a self-advocate. She commented, "Everything is possible in life. Trust in God. Set your goals and work hard toward them. You can accomplish whatever you want. You are the sole barrier to your own success." Her advice to other parents is "Always support your child and push them on. If they are struggling and consider giving in, then continue providing encouragement."

The past year, I met Ira and Chauncy for dinner at a local restaurant. Chauncy was no longer employed as a cook at the UTRGV cafeteria. He was now pursuing his lifelong dream of opening his own business and selling Native American arts and crafts and other items. He was also doing this to honor his father's Native American heritage.

Recalling his middle school and high school years and his unfortunate situation of being preyed on and bullied by other students, Chauncy realized he was different from other students and more mentally advanced. He told me, "I thought differently than them. Some took it as a challenge, and others thought of me as an easy target."

Chauncy's mild case of Asperger's made things difficult. He struggled with it. It was hard for him to distinguish other people's facial expressions, gestures, and mannerisms. He would not respond well to their insults, although he considered himself to be a pacifist and a nice kid.

Chauncy considers Asperger's to be both a blessing and a curse—a blessing in that he can envision and create different ideas and a curse in that it is difficult for him to understand certain social issues such as politics.

For others with a disability, Chauncy suggested, "Do not give up. Figure out what your best ability is and run with it. Focus on your strengths, and do not let others dictate your life."

To date, Ira still believes Chauncy is her miracle child. Her faith has enabled her to deal with Chauncy and with difficult issues in life such as the recent passing of her husband, Ruben.

It is by our tremendous faith that we expect a miracle! And many of us are fortunate to experience one.

A miracle can and will occur if we passionately believe it in our minds and fully trust in God and our Lord and Savior Jesus Christ.

Two years ago, I was fortunate to meet up with a Christian couple, Hilario and Ileana Gomez, who are the proud parents of Sammy, a ten-year-old child with Down syndrome. Hilario and Ileana have made it a priority to enable Sammy to participate in adaptive sporting events with the Capable Kids Foundation through Champions League Sports, Special Olympics, and other foundations.

Sammy is a lovable and outgoing child who lights up everyone's life. He loves to participate in different sporting events, especially baseball. His younger brother, Manny, loves baseball. Sammy is his greatest fan.

As a former coach and volunteer with the Capable Kids Foundation and Champions League Sports, I had the opportunity to coach Sammy in various adaptive sporting events. Sammy is an incredibly competitive athlete who always demonstrates teamwork. He loves the attention of the audience, especially the female volunteers, always wanting to hug them and kiss them on the cheek.

I wanted to know more about Sammy's Down syndrome and the other medical conditions he faced, so I decided to contact Hilario, who graciously accepted my request for an interview.

Hilario and Ileana dated for several years and were married in May 2007. Around three years after that, they decided to conceive a child. Ileana became pregnant in 2009 and had no serious issues during her pregnancy. According to Hilario, she only had some morning sickness, which occurred mostly in the evenings, along with mood changes. At five months pregnant, Ileana underwent several examinations and had blood work done at their pediatrician's office. To their surprise, the doctor was the bearer of sad news. He commented there was a high probability their child would be born with Down syndrome.

Hilario was OK with the news. However, Ileana was devastated by the potential outcome. It was their firstborn, and she was nervous and afraid of the unknown, not knowing what to expect or how to raise a child with special needs. A month prior to this, the couple had become aware their baby was a boy and decided to name him Sammy.

The doctors mentioned that the couple would have to wait until after the baby's birth to determine his true medical condition and the severity of the Down syndrome.

Hilario and Ileana prayed daily and decided to continue with the pregnancy and welcome their son into the world. Several months later, Ileana was admitted to Rio Grande Regional Hospital in McAllen, Texas, where she underwent seven painful hours of child labor. She gave natural birth to their newborn son, Samuel (Sammy), who was two weeks premature.

The doctor had a special team of medical experts on standby waiting for the birth of Sammy. Their subsequent medical examinations determined that one of the chambers/valves of Sammy's heart was leaking and needing to be operated on. After several days, Ileana and Sammy were discharged from the hospital. The following week, a visit to a cardiologist confirmed Sammy's delicate heart condition. Hilario and Ileana were faced with a dire situation. Sammy needed to be operated on, and soon, to enhance his life expectancy.

Hilario and Ileana prayed constantly for a miracle.

At four months of age, Sammy underwent a life-threatening heart procedure conducted by a pediatric cardiologist at Driscoll's Children's Hospital in Corpus Christ, Texas. Afterward, Sammy was placed in the intensive care unit because there was excessive fluid in one of his lungs. According to Hilario, it was an extremely nerve-wracking time, but their heartfelt prayers prevailed. Sammy was in God's hands and was recuperating from the procedure. After a month, he was discharged from the hospital, and they returned home.

Sammy was still in a fragile state and required extra care at home, including an oxygen mask. After a week, Sammy was gradually weaned off the oxygen. Hilario and Ileana continued praying for Sammy's recovery. Nothing else mattered to them in life but his well-being.

A follow-up examination with the pediatrician resulted in dreadful news they were not expecting to hear and were not at the time able to deal with. Because of Sammy's Down syndrome and heart condition, they were advised he might end up with a feeding tube and be unable to walk, run, or perform other daily functions.

Hilario declared, "What kept us going was a lot of prayers and our faith. Our faith kept us going. We had set a goal not to give up. We constantly prayed on and on."

Hilario and Ileana put their trust in the specialists/doctors who were caring for Sammy. The pressure was on them to perform this delicate surgery on Sammy, which ultimately proved successful.

Hilario and Ileana placed their entire lives in God's hands and trusted in His will! Nothing else mattered but the health of Sammy. Fortunately, Sammy recuperated and was able to function normally. His parents' faith and prayers had prevailed.

Sammy was able to walk at the age of two and had delayed speech. Still unable to speak correctly at age four, he required weekly therapy. Because of Sammy's delicate condition, his parents decided to care for him at home with their aunt pitching in to help. She pampered Sammy, and he took advantage of this. But his parents kept pushing him on.

Two years later, they placed Sammy in a day care center. He loved the environment and associating with other children. He was there for approximately two years. It had a positive influence on his personality.

After this, they placed Sammy, who was now four years, in a private pre-K school in McAllen. They later observed he had regressed quite a bit, to the point that he would soil on himself. Hilario and Ileana became overly concerned about Sammy's sudden deteriorating behavior. Prior to this, they had attended an orientation and voiced their concerns to the teachers and administrators about Sammy's condition. They were told not to worry, that the school had a great staff with special needs experience. When school started, Sammy began to soil himself and experienced other detrimental changes.

Hilario and Ileana were convinced the school staff were not paying enough attention to Sammy or providing him with proper care. Sammy was miserable, and his personality showed it.

Hilario and Ileana attended a meeting with the school's vice principal and again voiced their concerns about Sammy's behavior. They continued pressing for more information and at times were not told anything. They later met the vice principal yet again, who stated the school was doing everything they could to assist Sammy and also said they could not deal with him as he was a distraction to the other kids.

Allegedly Sammy's teacher had prior experience as a special education teacher dealing with special needs children. But Hilario did not believe the school. He pointed out, "The school was not up to par in providing the proper education and services to our son or the special needs community." He and his wife tried to schedule a meeting with the principal, but they were denied one. Hilario and Ileana were irate; they were being ignored. To their minds, the principal's refusal to meet with them showed an unquestionably demeaning attitude. And there were other issues the school was not addressing.

For example, a woman from a day care center had been hired to pick up Sammy after school and care for him. This was necessary as both Hilario and Ileana were working. On one occasion, the woman arrived at the school and saw Sammy alone sitting on a concrete table. She immediately brought this to the attention of a teacher on duty, who remarked, "He is not my student." This was a defining moment and the breaking point for Hilario and Ileana. They were primarily concerned for Sammy's well-being as the school was not giving him the required attention and was failing to give him a proper education.

After five weeks, the Gomezes made the drastic decision to enroll Sammy in a public school at the PSJA (Pharr–San Juan–Alamo) School District—particularly, Carmen Anaya School—for one year as recommended by the day care staff. They knew the public school setting would be beneficial for his development. Amazingly, Sammy became more outgoing, was more comfortable, smiled a lot, and wanted to associate with other kids. The change was a positive one for him. Hilario declared, "It was like night and day. The change was astonishing. Sammy changed into a different person. He loved going to school."

At the age of five, Sammy was enrolled at a different school located in the city of Pharr. The administration treated Sammy politely. The principal took the initiative to offer special education courses as part of the curriculum to assist Sammy and others. Sammy happily continued attending school and making new friends. He took several hours of special education courses and then took regular class courses the rest of the day.

Hilario and Ileana made sure Sammy underwent occupational and speech therapy in school each week to assist him in life.

In spring 2015, Sammy, at the age of four, began competing

in adaptive sporting events with Champions League Sports sponsored by the nonprofit Capable Kids Foundation. This was the first time I had had the opportunity to meet Hilario, Ileana, Sammy, and his younger brother. Sammy was smiling and eager to join his teammates in an adaptive basketball game. He was wearing the uniform of his favorite team, the Chicago Bulls, and the color red. His competitive drive was evident during the game as Sammy smiled and jumped for joy after scoring a basket.

Several years later, Sammy began to compete with other athletes at Special Olympics sporting events. He also continued playing adaptive basketball, football, soccer, and baseball with Champions League Sports.

I was fortunate to coach Sammy for several of those games and consider him to be a fine athlete. Sammy loved the crowd and would wave his hands toward them to cheer everyone on. He exhibited true teamwork and compassion for his teammates. Through the years, Sammy received numerous medals and trophies, which are now proudly displayed in his bedroom.

I will never forget my lengthy hospital stays in San Antonio and Houston battling cancer. I was constantly encouraged by Sammy's telephone calls. Sammy and his parents would call my wife and me several times a week and pray with us. I will never forget Sammy's gracious words: "Do not worry, Coach Al. You are going to be fine. I love you, and Jesus loves you. We are praying for your recovery. We love you."

Those tender words of encouragement melted my heart and caused me to shed tears. The love of an innocent child like Sammy made me figure out I was loved and needed. I became very aware that I was not fighting only for my life but also for my wife, sons, family members, and friends.

Sammy always demonstrates kindness and love toward others, mostly during sporting events. He is like a little spark plug who continuously keeps plugging away and smiling. According to Hilario and Ileana, he will always be their miracle child and a blessing from God.

We must always remember that miracles can happen. These supernatural events can and will produce healing. It is our profound faith and trust in God that enables this.

A miracle!

God heals!

Believe in God and He will embrace you with His grace and heal you.

The Holy Scriptures indicate that God's Word is healing, as noted in Psalm 107:30: "He sent His word, and healed them, and rescued them from their destruction" (AMP).

The other day, my wife and I went out for a quiet dinner. During this precious time together, she voiced her concerns about my health, saying, "You are a miracle from God. You have survived cancer. Not everyone survives cancer, and many who do are "scarred for life." They are changed forever and see life differently and appreciate the small things in life. You are a survivor! Don't go on in life doubting yourself or being depressed. Be grateful for another beautiful day. We all love you! And most important of all, God loves you!"

My firm belief is that my surviving cancer was a miracle with God giving me a second chance in life. Every day God continues to perform outright miracles in the lives of countless human beings. What a remarkable phenomenon! God is larger than life! He has a plan for everyone.

If you believe, then miracles will happen in your life. Train your mind to think positive thoughts, and then your thoughts will become reality and result in positive outcomes. Just believe, keep the faith, and trust in God!

CHAPTER 6

KEEP PRAYING

Be careful, for nothing; but in everything by prayer and supplication with thanksgiving let your requests be made known unto God.

—Philippians 4:6

Prayer is one of the ways by which we communicate directly with God and Jesus Christ, a moment of solitude when we express our desires and confess our sins. We worship God in a fixed spot or a special place of our own choosing, a quiet and peaceful place to worship the Father.

But questions arise about prayer and its meaning: Why do people pray? What is the true meaning of prayer? How does prayer benefit us? These and many more questions have been asked by many people for centuries.

In praying, we make a fervent petition and give thanks and praise to our God.

According to the Old and New Testament of the Bible, prayer is a loving relationship with God. We praise God, worship Him, and thank Him for all His blessings. In praying, not only should we converse with God, but also we must listen to Him.

In our Christian faith and in many other spiritual traditions, prayer is the primary method we have for developing an intimate and spiritual relationship with God. It is also a way of relating to God by making our praise and requests known to Him.[1]

We must understand this is the direct line of communication to God, intimate and precious time when we are one-on-one with Him. A valuable Bible verse supporting this idea is Mark 11:24, which reads, "Therefore I tell you, whatever you ask in prayer, believe that you have received it, and it will be yours" (NIV).

My wife and I met Maricruz Costilla at one of our monthly support group meetings with AWARE-RGV. Maricruz is a sincere person, a devoted wife, and a caring mother of four children. We consider her an ardent believer in God and a model of a righteous praying woman. Her oldest child, Danny, age fourteen, is an outgoing and somewhat reserved kid who has Down syndrome. Maricruz resided in Mexico with her husband and had a wonderful pregnancy with no issues. She would travel and visit family members and a doctor in the United States, but her ultimate plan was to stay in Mexico.

Maricruz attended a doctor's appointment in the United States and was informed by a nurse that examinations had revealed the baby had several medical complications such as fluid in his brain and kidney and liver problems and that he was going to die. She was transported to a local hospital, McAllen Medical Center in McAllen, Texas, and underwent an emergency C-section, resulting in the birth of her son Danny in October 2007. The first words out of the doctor's mouth were, "He has Down. He has Down syndrome." Maricruz was curious what he meant by *Down* and why he was telling her this. It did not bother her though. She only wanted her child to be healthy. She begged to get a glimpse of him, but he was immediately taken away. Maricruz recalls doctors saying her son would live for only a few hours because of several medical complications. She was distraught. What could be wrong with him? What did he have? Although Maricruz feared the worst, she prayed to God and kept her faith.

Maricruz's husband mentioned he had been approached by several hospital doctors and nurses who indicated he should prepare for the worst. The child was expected to survive for only an hour. Maricruz and her husband braced themselves for the worst outcome.

After birth, Danny was placed in an incubator in the intensive care unit. Maricruz visited him the following day and saw that his breathing was being aided by an oxygen mask. His recovery was slow, lasting about fifteen days. During this time, the doctors and nurses provided Maricruz with daily updates on Danny's medical condition and any improvements.

Maricruz's dad initially visited the family in the hospital after Danny's birth. All the family members were talking about the child being sick and having Down syndrome. Maricruz commented to me, "No one in my family or in my husband's family had ever encountered anyone with Down syndrome. It was not an issue to me."

Maricruz spoke with her father, and he said, "The child is going to be fine. Don't worry about it. The child is going to be fine. I prayed to the Virgin and made a promise. The child will be fine." Maricruz recalls telling her dad one thing. She became emotional remembering their conversation. In a cracking voice, she uttered, "I prayed to God and thanked God. He heard me. I thank God. He has always heard me. It does not make me sad; on the contrary, it gives me an extraordinary amount of joy to know God was always with us. I told Dad, 'No, Daddy, my son is cured.' But my father did not understand me or comprehend what Down syndrome was. It was as if my father didn't understand and believed the baby was sick."

Maricruz responded to her dad, "My child was fine before birth. Maybe before he was born God decided to change him. It was His plan all along to change him. Dad, I do not care if Danny has Down syndrome. I love him a lot, with all my heart. The only thing I pleaded to God about was to give me a healthy son. I do not care if he has Down syndrome, as long as he is in good health. That is why I get sentimental, because God heard me. I am fine with it. I thank God my son does not have anything wrong. I am aware children with Down syndrome have heart issues, but it does not bother me. My son does not have any other health issues whatsoever."

Maricruz was discharged from the hospital and refused to leave her child behind. It caused her grief and stressed her to be away from him. She could not imagine how other mothers were able to deal with a situation like hers. She asked herself, *How can I leave without my child? How can I leave him behind alone?*

Maricruz told me, "Oh my God, it was a dreadful situation. Every day was torment. I would be at home crying all the time. But I was able to visit my son at the hospital daily. I would be accompanied by my mother, and we would stay there from around eight o'clock in the morning to half past six in the evening. When the nurses were changing shifts, I had to go back home. If I could have stayed with him all day and night, I would have, but I had to be home and recover from my C-section surgery."

After Danny was discharged from the hospital, his parents took him home, and the family celebrated his recovery.

I asked Maricruz what her husband thought about the child's condition, and she replied that he was fine with it.

Maricruz recalls being at her in-laws' home and sitting down in a chair at the dinner table, holding Danny in her arms, and staring at a statue of the Virgin of Guadalupe. Thoughts raced through her mind, and she began to cry. Thinking of the future, she asked herself, *What am I going to do? How am I going to do it? How is my son going to be? Is he going to be able to speak? Is he going to be able to walk and clothe himself?* "Many questions raced through my mind," she said to me. "How am I going to get through this?"

Maricruz's husband came up to her and stared directly into

her eyes. He asked, "What is wrong with you, babe? Why are you crying?"

She responded, "It's because I'm thinking of my son. How he is going to do things when he grows up? Is he going to be able to walk and talk? And then what about school given the way other kids are cruel and mean?"

Her husband responded firmly, "Don't cry, and don't worry. He will not suffer. He is not going to suffer. That's why he has us. Our son is going to be fine. He has our unconditional love."

Maricruz exclaimed, "I felt like a veil had been removed from my head and mind. I was at peace. This was the last time I cried for my son."

Danny thereafter required special attention by a cardiologist, a pulmonologist, and a pediatric geneticist. He was born with a small hole in his heart and at four months old underwent a successful procedure. Maricruz indicated this heart condition is prevalent among people who are born with Down syndrome.

A prominent pediatrician friend of ours confirmed Maricruz's statement. In his experience dealing with children with Down syndrome, he has discovered issues with their cardiovascular systems. More than half the infants with Down syndrome are born with holes in their hearts.

Maricruz made a life-changing decision and gave up her career in Mexico, where she was employed as a registered nurse supervising a local hospital's surgery department. Maricruz declared, "Our entire lives changed after the birth of my son. I gave up my job, and my husband gave up his. We left Mexico and decided to stay in the United States to provide Danny with the best medical care. We praise God the change was for the best."

As a young child, Danny required three types of therapy several times a week. He would undergo occupational, physical, and speech therapy to help him cope in life. These therapies assisted him in developing his sensory and motor skills.

Maricruz commented, "To parent a child with special needs

is demanding work that requires patience. Because of Danny's condition, he requires a lot of attention and love. I have devoted my entire life to him, and I love him deeply."

Danny is the type who likes to hug people, but at times he refuses to hug certain individuals. When questioned why this is so, he responded, "*Malo* [bad]," meaning that he gets bad vibes from some people and senses no love in them. Thus, he tends to shy away and avoid such people.

Maricruz grew up as a Catholic and made sure Danny followed that same path by completing his First Communion. She taught him to pray to God and pray for other individuals such as his family members and friends. She once asked Danny about God and His love, and he responded, "God my Father is in my heart. I love Him, and He loves me."

Danny is kindhearted and expresses his love for others by being considerate and praying for them. During my time associating with Danny at various adaptive sporting events under the auspices of Champions League Sports, he exhibited genuine kindness and respect for other participants.

Maricruz conveyed to her son that he should have faith in God and be unquestionably thankful for His blessings. She taught Danny good moral values and respect for others. She pointed out, "It is up to us as parents to educate our kids, teach them moral values, teach them how to pray, and educate them in table manners and hygiene. It is no one else's responsibility but ours as parents. There are no excuses!"

Danny takes his hygiene seriously, and he likes to be well-dressed in jeans, a western-style shirt and boots, and a cowboy hat and to wear men's cologne. He is a very sociable person who loves to be around his fellow students and friends at school. He does not allow his condition to prevent him from attending regular sixth grade classes at the Vanguard Academy. He adores music, specifically Mexican *ranchera* songs and mariachi.

On October 4, 2019, Danny's lifelong dream of meeting his

music idol came true. My wife, through her contacts, set up a once-in-a-lifetime meeting between Danny and the famous young Mexican music star Christian Nodal. This special meeting took place backstage at the McAllen, Texas, Performing Arts Center. It was a surprise gift for Danny's twelfth birthday and his best birthday ever. His prayers were about to come true!

A local television station, Channel 40, Telemundo, recorded the special meeting between Danny and Christian prior to Christian's concert. During their exchange, Danny presented Christian with a gift box with a Batman figurine in it and also a box of Godiva chocolates. Christian was impressed by Danny's gesture, and in return he autographed Danny's guitar. They both hugged several times and jointly sang one of Christian's most popular songs, "Adios Amor" (Goodbye Love). This debut single earned Christian notoriety and enabled him to break into the music marked in the United States, Mexico, and other Latin American countries.

In 2017, Christian was nominated for and awarded Best Song and Best New Artist at the Latin American Music Awards and Bandamax Music Awards, with more nominations received for the Radio Music Awards. In 2018, he received more nominations and awards at the Billboard Latin Music Awards and the iHeartRadio Music Awards. In 2019, Christian won Regional Mexican Artist of the Year at the Billboard Latin Music Awards.[2]

One evening, my wife and I received a telephone call from Maricruz, who was exceedingly delighted and overcome with excitement. She repeatedly thanked us for Danny's special birthday gift. After several days passed, we spoke to her again, and she indicated Danny was still excited and overcome with joy, unable to sleep at night. He was in awe and in shock after receiving the gift of a lifetime. Since then, Danny has shown enthusiasm for playing the accordion.

Danny continues to be involved in extracurricular activities and participates in adaptive sporting events such as baseball, basketball, soccer, and football sponsored by Champions League Sports (Capable Kids Foundation, Special Olympics, and Hidalgo County, Texas, precinct #2). His striking enthusiasm brings joy to his family members and to other participants.

Currently, Danny uses a special pillow that converts music into vibrations (a Dreampad) to calm his anxiety as recommended by one of his therapists. Danny also utilizes noise-canceling headphones to dial out people's voices and other loud noises when the family is out in public or at a social event. If he doesn't do this, he experiences sensory overload, resulting in anxiety and a strong urge to run away and be alone.

Because of the coronavirus stay-at-home orders, schools were canceled for the rest of 2020 in South Texas. However, Maricruz began homeschooling Danny and providing him with physical therapy, occupational therapy, and other therapies via Zoom. She continues to care for Danny and keeps praying to God to keep him safe. Maricruz's strong faith in God enables her to continue in life, battling any adversity she and Danny encounter. She told me, "I have no ill will toward God, and I thank Him daily for Danny's well-being and every beautiful day I enjoy with my family."

We must continue praying daily for our health and the well-being of loved ones. But the question sometimes arises, how do we pray?

Our best example for how to pray was given to us by Our Lord and Savior Jesus Christ, who taught His disciples the proper way to pray. In Matthew 6:6, Christ says, "But when you pray, go into your room, close the door, and pray to your Father [God], who is unseen. Then your Father, who sees what is done in secret, will reward you" (NIV). Being alone with God is ideal, a spiritual sanctuary. We thus worship God in spirit and truth.

Jesus went further when discussing the correct way to pray to God. He declared in Matthew 6:9, "Our Father in heaven, hallowed be your name, your kingdom come, your will be done on earth as it is in heaven. Give us today our daily bread. Forgive us our debts, as we also have forgiven our debtors. And lead us not into temptation but deliver us from the evil one" (NIV).

This you will recognize as the Lord's Prayer, also mentioned in Luke 11:2–4. It has been used for centuries. Jesus discussed this as part of His Sermon on the Mount, which He delivered to a crowd of five thousand people.

Our prayers to God and Jesus Christ must be definite and spoken with faith.

C. S. Lewis was a committed atheist who spoke out against God. He was also a brilliant scholar who graduated from Oxford University in England. Finally having met his match in 1929 at the ripe age of thirty-one, he made a drastic life-changing decision. Lewis conceded and accepted God as the one true God. At this time, he knelt and began to pray. What an amazing and life-changing event![3]

Two years later, Lewis was taking a late-night stroll with several of his friends, and they all had a conversation. This event drastically changed him too. He became an ardent believer in Christianity. He went on to write numerous books on Christianity, in fact.

After that, Lewis went on to become a one of the twentieth century's leading defenders of God. He was a bestselling author of more than thirty books, an influential writer who explained the Christian faith. One of his most important books is entitled *How to Pray—Reflections & Essays*, which provides wisdom on prayer and its significance in our daily lives.

Another well-known Christian writer is Andrew Murray, who lived and ministered as a pastor in many villages and small towns in South Africa. His central belief and priority is prayer. Many people in our society do not pray. Thus, he advocated that prayer should be ingrained in our daily lives and take place in our homes and schools.

Murray emphasized our need to understand prayer and its

importance. He mentioned our need to practice praying. He ministered to thousands of people and authored more than fifty books.

With prayer, we can get closer to God and seek His guidance and support. God is always ready to hear our prayers. We must believe God cares for us and hears our prayers. No matter what situation we are in, we should confide and trust in God.

As founders of Aware Rio Grande Valley, a nonprofit organization, my wife and I were afforded the opportunity to meet various parents whose children had been diagnosed with different types of disabilities. One of these mothers, Nena Almaguer, is a strong believer in the power of prayer. She exhibits an intense love and compassion for her son, Miguel. During one of our parenting sessions, I spoke with Nena concerning her son's condition. She was glad to share her inspiring life story with me.

Nena began by talking about the birth of her one and only son, Miguel Almaguer, in 1996—a healthy seven-pound baby boy born at a medical center in McAllen. Miguel was a normal child and later developed into a highly intelligent student who received several academic awards at school. He was active, outgoing, and sociable and was highly creative in designing different crafts. During the weekends, he would accompany Nena to a local flea market in Brownsville, Texas, where he would sell arts and crafts, his own toys, and other items. According to Nena, "Miguel had a knack for socializing with people and selling assorted items. He was a businessperson at heart."

When Miguel reached the age of eight, a devastating event changed his life. He contracted an unknown virus and became seriously ill with severe headaches and vomiting. Nena struggled, taking him to several hospitals for a medical examination. The doctors disclosed that Miguel was having these severe migraine headaches and depression because his parents were divorcing. They placed him on a diet, but he continued vomiting and experiencing severe migraines.

Nena declared, "Miguel continued being sick for fifteen days with no cure. I became frustrated and decided to take him to a doctor in Mexico." The doctor examined Miguel and concluded it was not migraines or depression and that there was something much more serious wrong with the boy. He assumed it was a neurological condition and that Miguel might have contracted meningitis, a serious disease that causes inflammation of the brain and spinal cord. The doctor was unsure of his diagnosis as it was getting late, and he did not have a technician on-site to conduct the proper tests. Nena was disappointed and returned home with Miguel.

The following day, Miguel was unable to go to the bathroom and failed to speak to or even recognize Nena. Something was seriously affecting Miguel neurologically as he was not responding to her. Nena was in tears and extremely concerned about his deteriorating condition.

She took him to their family doctor for another visit, but it proved useless, the doctor prescribing several medications and caffeine for Miguel's severe headaches and nausea. After arriving home, Miguel's condition worsened. He was in constant agony. He had trouble speaking, made only sounds, and was unable to get himself out of bed as he was frail.

The following morning, Nena was hesitant to take Miguel to the local hospital because of her past negative experiences with no results. Later that afternoon, she drove Miguel to the doctor as his condition had deteriorated. The doctor notified the hospital, and Nena immediately transported Miguel to the hospital's emergency department, where she filled out all the paperwork for his admittance. Unbeknownst to her, and spontaneously, Miguel had passed out in the waiting room. He appeared pale and was gasping for air. His life was gradually fading away. Nurses and other medical personnel immediately rushed in and hastily took him away. Nena was unaware of the gravity of the situation. Miguel was in the intensive care unit fighting for his life.

The following morning, one of the medical staff members approached Nena and stated that he was the person who initially treated Miguel. He somberly declared, "I was in the emergency room, and my first patient was Miguel. I had to resuscitate him because he momentarily died [stopped breathing]."

Nena was in shock and distraught. No words came from her mouth.

What was wrong with Miguel? How could this have happened to him? What an astonishing revelation as her son had momentarily been dead!

Nena was heartbroken and crying for the life of her beloved son, a caring mother showing empathy and compassion for her son. There was nothing else she could do but place Miguel in the protective hands of Almighty God. From this moment forward, Nena began to pray earnestly for Miguel's well-being. She did not want to lose him. He was young and had a full life ahead of him.

Nena later received dreadful news. The doctors said that Miguel had a life-threatening disease called encephalitis, which causes confusion, convulsions, seizures, and other complications. A virus had entered his system and left him with partial brain damage, including physical problems, memory problems, personality changes, and speech issues. According to Nena, Miguel was a total mess experiencing constant convulsions like epileptic seizures. To the best of her knowledge, Miguel was resuscitated a handful of times by the medical staff. The heart-wrenching news of Miguel's life-threatening condition was agonizing for her. He was in a fierce battle to survive.

Nena recalls one occasion when Miguel stopped breathing and all the equipment alarms were going off in the room. Several nurses and other practitioners immediately rushed into the room to resuscitate Miguel, who had stopped breathing. It was a nightmarish experience for Nena. She commented, "It was my faith in God that kept me going. I knew deep inside me that God would heal Miguel. Almighty God is all-powerful and works miracles. I never gave up on Miguel."

Nena assumed Miguel had contracted the virus that caused his encephalitis while on a weekend vacation in San Antonio, Texas. Miguel and other friends were near the San Antonio River Walk, where the water is murky and stagnant with a lot of mosquitoes. She assumed Miguel acquired the virus one of two ways: (1) a mosquito bit Miguel and transferred the virus or (2) Miguel dipped his hand in the murky water of the river and then touched his face.

After they returned home from the hospital, the following day Miguel was bedridden, vomiting constantly with severe headaches and intense pain. He was in agony!

Every day Nena stayed by Miguel's bedside, gently holding his hand, talking to him, and praying to God. She said that Miguel would be convulsing and in severe pain, which was heart-wrenching for her to see. He was constantly medicated to ease the pain and calm him down. Nena exclaimed, "On several occasions, I had to get on top of Miguel and hold him down when he was convulsing to avoid additional damage to his brain and/ or body. This was painful and traumatic, something I will never forget for the rest of my life."

Here we have an excellent display of a mother following her instincts to help her suffering child. Nena is a mother willing to sacrifice everything and put in the extra effort to save her child.

Miguel was hospitalized for a month in the intensive care unit and subsequently was flown to the Children's Hospital in Houston, Texas, for further observation. Nena stayed by Miguel's side for the entire month, not wanting to leave him alone as she feared the worst.

Nena commented, "During our hospital stay, I saw Miguel stop breathing on several occasions, and they revived him. It was difficult to endure these life-and-death moments. I arrived at a point where I felt the agony and pain he was suffering. I thought of telling the doctors to just let him go when he stopped breathing. But deep down inside me, my maternal instincts urged me on. I could not give up. I would not give up on him. I still had hope and faith in God. He would heal Miguel."

Miguel was stabilized and gradually improved to the point that he was discharged from the hospital. He was subsequently admitted to a rehabilitation center, where he was closely guarded by nurses and underwent daily physical therapy treatments for fifteen days before being discharged.

As Nena tells it, "Miguel would stutter and speak like a child and use certain words. He was like a baby. I had to teach him again how to eat, drink, and walk. He had braces on his legs and began to walk calmly with our assistance."

Nena also told me, "I always opened the Bible to Psalm 23 and Psalm 91 and prayed these verses prior to Miguel undergoing any medical procedures. I would question God, asking, 'When will my child get better and be in good health?' But I never gave up hope or lost faith. The Bible I read was Miguel's personal Precious Moments Bible translated into Spanish. At the time I didn't have my own personal Bible, so I used his to pray to God. I believe God wanted me to get closer to Him. There is a reason for what happened to Miguel. God knows. He has a purpose for both of us."

Nena continued, saying, "I believed God would never drop me from His caring hands. Prior to the birth of Miguel, several doctors told me I would never get pregnant or have children. The birth of my son was a miracle. Besides Miguel, I was blessed with a second child, a wonderful daughter who loves him dearly." Nena considered Miguel's recuperation to be a second miracle, a special gift from God in His grace!

At home, Nena cared daily for Miguel with the assistance of a nurse and her daughter. He was intubated with a G-tube and used an oxygen cannula. He became anorexic and was in a vegetative state for about one and a half years. He could not speak, hear, or recognize anyone. Nena was distressed and felt useless. She continuously asked herself, *Will my son ever regain consciousness, or will he remain in a vegetative state the rest of his life? What must I do to make him get better?*

Nena is a mentally strong woman who never lost faith and has a positive outlook on life. She always prayed and hoped for the best for her son. Her trust was in God!

Family members and friends would question her about Miguel's recovery. She always replied the same way: "Miguel is going to get better and be able to perform like a regular kid. I am aware. God is working on it. I have hope and faith! Miguel is going to get better, and he will recover. I strongly believe this to be true!"

Nena made sure Miguel had different toys and trinkets around him, and she played classical music to stimulate his brain. Although he had no sense of sight, these items and others stimulated his sense of touch.

A feeding tube and oxygen mask were the main necessities for Miguel's survival. He was in a fight for his life, struggling to survive this dreadful disease. He was in God's powerful hands!

One day, a cable repair person was at Nena's home fixing the cable line to the television. He glanced over at Miguel, who was lying in bed. Miguel had turned his head to the side toward the sound from the television. The cable repair person immediately informed Nena of this. Nena was in disbelief when Miguel opened his eyes and partially smiled. He was now able to notice her, hear her, and make small noises with his mouth. Nena was in tears, praising and thanking God.

Nena said to me, "It was a miracle! God healed Miguel and made him better. My prayers had been answered. I knew deep down inside he would be healed. Our loving God is the answer! I never gave up my hope and faith! We have a loving God!"

Miguel later began the slow and arduous process of learning

to walk, taking small steps like a baby. He slowly began coming out of his chrysalis like a butterfly, albeit still in pain. After his recovery, Miguel participated in occupational, physical, and speech therapy several times a week, along with sensory therapy (music) four times a week. He was prescribed seven different prescription medications, which he took daily to control his aggressiveness, calm his anxiety, and prevent convulsions.

Nena declared, "It was the most demanding time of my life. My faith is what kept me going. I hope he gets better and recuperates. I never lost my faith. I would stay positive and say every day, 'He is going to get better. He is going to get up and walk. He is going to be fine.' People would question my resolve, but I didn't care. I stayed positive. I always prayed to God for Miguel's health. Firmly, God worked on Miguel. And yes, Miguel got better!'"

I asked Nena how a person should act when faced with such adversity. She modestly replied, "Most importantly, when faced with a situation like this, one must always stay positive. One must keep faith, hope, and trust in God. No one else can help you out but God. He is the powerful and almighty God. Put all your faith and trust in Him. God will provide for you and help you!"

Miguel continued his rehabilitation therapy with several therapists. At times he became overly aggressive and lashed out at the therapists, at Nena, and at others around him. The virus had seriously affected his neurological system, and he was unable to control his aggression and anger. At times he behaved like a wild animal. The medications were the primary solution to keep him calm and relaxed. Without the medications, he was uncontrollable, like a raging bull.

Nena decided to try other, unconventional therapies to assist Miguel in his recovery. One therapist recommended craniosacral therapy, which Nena in turn researched and agreed to try out. The therapist described craniosacral therapy as a gentle direct technique that works with the soft tissues of the body to assist the flow of cerebrospinal fluid between the head and the base of the spine. By applying this therapy on Miguel, it relieved the tension in his central nervous system, relieved his pain, and promoted a sense of well-being.

However, this alternative treatment had a high cost of fifty-nine hundred dollars for five daylong therapy sessions provided at a facility located in Palm Beach, Florida. Nena was strapped for money and did not have the funds to afford this treatment. She gratefully obtained assistance from family members and friends, raising money at barbecue benefits and other charitable events.

A close friend who was taking a vacation to Florida offered to provide the family with transportation to Palm Beach at no cost. Nena was grateful and accepted the offer. Nena and Miguel thereafter accompanied this friend on the long journey to Florida.

Miguel's first day of therapy was successful. He began to walk alone without any assistance, taking several steps forward and backward. He continued therapy for the entire week, from Monday to Friday, responding positively to the therapies and appearing livelier and more energetic. Nena thanked God for this small step forward.

Nena and Miguel left Florida and arrived home several days later. At home, Miguel continued with his therapies, including hydrotherapy, which over time proved beneficial to his physical health. Nena kept Miguel grounded at home because of his bad temper and aggression, often lashing out and hitting others. On one occasion, she enrolled him in school for two months but had to remove him because of his anger problem. Unfortunately, the virus had seriously affected Miguel's brain and his entire neurological system. He was permanently damaged! There was no cure. Prescription medications were still the solution to keep him functioning and stable.

Besides his regular therapies, Miguel wore a weighted vest

to calm him down and a helmet to avoid any potential head injury. Nena sacrificed her career and began homeschooling Miguel on her own. She taught him how to read and write from various schoolbooks she had purchased. Over time, Miguel began to understand more, socialize, and develop into an active person. Unfortunately, he never attended classes in person or online because of his poor physical condition, his psychological impairment, and his family's dire financial situation.

After several years passed, Miguel began to participate in private kung fu lessons. He subsequently enrolled in the Texas Family Martial Arts Academy in McAllen under the tutelage of Shifu Israel Flores, a black belt. Nena made sure Miguel continued with his training for two years. According to her, the adaptive methods of kung fu helped Miguel gain discipline, confidence, a sense of security, and understanding.

I can personally attest to this as a close relative, Alex, an Aspie, likewise attended kung fu classes with Shifu Flores and other children and young adults with disabilities. The training made a positive impact on Alex's athletic ability and also increased his self-confidence and self-discipline, changing him for the better.

During the fall of 2015, my wife and I were active members of Champions League Sports. We had the pleasure of meeting Nena and Miguel for the first time at a baseball park located in south McAllen during the fall season. Miguel participated in this event, playing adaptive baseball with other kids and young adults with different types of disabilities. He was ecstatic to play and to meet other players and eventually develop friendships with them. Throughout the year, he played other sports, such as adaptive basketball, soccer, football, and bowling.

As a coach with Champions League Sports, I had the privilege of coaching kids and young adults with various disabilities and associating with their parents. One of the young adults who stood out among all the other participants was Miguel. He was outgoing, constantly smiling, generous to others, and most of all incredibly competitive. His big smile always brought joy to others.

Besides prescription medications, Miguel takes homeopathic medicines. He participates in recreational therapy and painting lessons. Nena recently enrolled him in hippotherapy with horses as a therapeutic treatment. This therapy has been used effectively to improve motor skills, neurological function, and sensory processes in persons such as Miguel who have autism and other types of disorders or disabilities. Nena is very confident about this therapy as she has seen the positive results for Miguel. He has changed for the better and now understands more concepts.

I asked Nena what recommendation she would make to parents who have children with disabilities. She firmly replied, "Do not lose your faith. Be confident, stay positive, and most of all trust in God. Everything will work out for the best."

In March 2020, I was fortunate to receive a personal gift from Miguel, an eight-by-ten oil painting of two hands folded in prayer. I became emotional from his nice gesture. I found the painting a perfect home: it is proudly displayed on my nightstand next to my bed. I am extremely honored to own this painting. I will always treasure this sentimental gift.

Many of us forget to pray daily and instead use prayer primarily as a crutch to assist us whenever we encounter something challenging and troubling. We then plead for God's or Jesus Christ's help to alleviate any pain or hardship we are going through, or to solve a challenging problem, or to deal with a life-threatening incident. We fail to follow Christ's instruction and open a line for intimate communication with God.

We should make prayer a habit. Better yet, we should make a formal commitment to pray.

Prayer! Pray continuously! Pray daily and on all occasions.

The apostle Paul writes in 1 Thessalonians 5:16–18, "Rejoice evermore, pray without ceasing. In everything give thanks: for this is the will of God in Christ Jesus concerning you." In Philippians

4:6, he says, "Do not be anxious or worried about anything, but in everything by prayer and petition with thanksgiving, continue to make your requests known to God."

Additionally, make it a daily habit to pray to God and thank Him for His blessings.

CHAPTER 7

NEVER GIVE UP

Let not your heart be troubled; ye believe (trust)
in God, believe (trust) also in me.

—John 14:1

Everyone on earth has encountered adversity and challenges in their lifetimes. These drastic events affect us in more ways than one. They define the way we behave.

Many people easily succumb to these challenges without putting up much of a fight. But others take on the challenge with vigor, fighting relentlessly with a strong will and determination to succeed. Such people have a positive outlook on life and a strong will to survive.

The most famous female tennis player of all time is Martina Navratilova, from the Czech Republic. At the ripe age of eighteen, she asked the United States for political asylum and was granted temporary residence.

In 2005, *Tennis* magazine selected her as the best female tennis player for the years 1975–2005, and she is considered one of the best female tennis players of all time. Navratilova is a Hall of Famer and eighteen-time Grand Slam winner who also won numerous other titles such as Wimbledon, the US Open, and the French Open.

Throughout her life and after her marvelous tennis career, Navratilova faced many challenges. In 2010, she was up against a most devastating opponent, cancer, having been diagnosed with breast cancer and undergoing chemotherapy. Navratilova is a cancer survivor who shares her ordeal with others. She is quoted as saying, "Life is about challenges and how we face up to them and the attitude we take into everyday life, so hopefully we'll be able to motivate people to do more with their life."[1]

Recently, another female tennis star, Chris Evert, was diagnosed with ovarian cancer. Navratilova immediately voiced her support for Evert. Both tennis legends are facing the same dreadful rival: cancer. But with their "never give up" and winning attitudes, they will prevail.

The adversity and challenges we face in life end up shaping our character. We must also adopt a "never give up" attitude when confronted with such obstacles. We can overcome life's challenges by staying strong and fighting on.

My wonderful mom once provided advice on how to overcome challenges and succeed in life. She said, "You must work hard, sacrifice, be determined, think positively, and most important of all keep the faith and refuse to give up."

I have used these techniques in life, especially when faced with adversities such as battling cancer, among other medical problems and personal issues. It has proven successful, and I highly recommend it to everyone.

Over the years, I have met several individuals who have adopted a "never give up" attitude when faced with adversity. The following story is of a young man with disabilities who is a fine example of adopting this frame of mind.

In 2015, my wife and I had the privilege of meeting numerous children and young adults and their families who were part of AWARE RGV, a nonprofit organization established to assist people who have autism. This organization's primary goal is to provide resources and education for the autism community of the

Rio Grande Valley in South Texas. They host monthly support groups geared toward providing education and moral support to families living with a loved one who has autism. Esmeralda and other members of AWARE-RGV also team up with different nonprofit organizations to support people afflicted with other disabilities.

One of the young adults we were fortunate enough to meet and associate with was a Hispanic male named Lorenzo Tijerina from Mission, Texas. Lorenzo was brought up by two loving parents with his brother and two sisters. He is the youngest child and the tallest in the family. Lorenzo recalls his mother telling him how as a child with a high fever he was taken to a local hospital in an ambulance. Lorenzo said, "The high fever affected me, causing me to develop a speech impediment, crooked bones / arthritis, learning disabilities, and other things. I was never the same. My life totally changed."

From elementary school through middle school, Lorenzo was assigned to a special education class with other students who had similar disabilities. He later underwent speech therapy and physical therapy to help him communicate and cope with others. During those demanding school years, he experienced both good and bad days. Lorenzo describes a dreadful day as one where he was constantly verbally abused or bullied by several of his fellow students. They would make fun of him by calling him names and mocking him because of his speech impediment.

Lorenzo remembers one occasion when a female student purposely tripped him and he fell to the ground, scraping both knees. But instead of allowing these bullies to keep him down, he adopted a more positive outlook on life. Lorenzo's faith in God and his deep inner drive motivated him to stay strong.

Lorenzo overcame the challenges he faced in school and successfully graduated from Juarez Lincoln High School in 2012. He believed in something much greater than himself and refused to allow his impairments or disability to take him down. His previous experiences in his early school years as a victim of constant belittling and bullying by his fellow students had taught him a lesson and made him take a different approach to life. Lorenzo claimed, "During my middle school years, I rebelled and hung out with a different crowd who accepted me for who I was. They helped me speak up and have a stronger voice in life."

Lorenzo proclaimed, "I never give up. No matter what the challenges are or what I face, I will keep moving forward in life and getting up to face any adversity."

Several years after this, Lorenzo made numerous friends while participating as an athlete with Champions League Sports under the umbrella of the nonprofit Capable Kids Foundation. During this time, I had the opportunity to coach Lorenzo and associate with him on and off the field. I saw he displayed a positivity toward life and liked other people. Lorenzo, who was the tallest among all the players, felt welcomed by the other participants, who had either similar or different disabilities. He considers his fellow athletes and friends to be his second family.

Currently, Lorenzo spends his time taking photographs and making YouTube videos about life in general. He believes in God and prays every day for his family members, his friends, and himself. I asked Lorenzo if he had any recommendations for anybody, and he answered, "Be yourself, always smile, and never give up. You have to continue going on. He further said, "Every day is an adventure, and life is too short."

Never giving up reflects our true character. We must stay focused, be positive, keep our faith, and stay strong. Nothing will ever be easy in life. But our resolve will help us succeed and overcome any obstacles.

I am convinced the famous Hollywood action star Sylvester Stallone embraced a "never give up" attitude while pursuing his lifelong dream of becoming an actor. Stallone worked at all sorts of odd jobs and made sacrifices to make a living. It was his tough mindset, his determination, and his enthusiasm, never giving up, that enabled him to succeed in life. He became one of Hollywood's most famous actors and starred in various successful action films such as *Rocky*, *Rambo*, and *The Expendables*, among others.

I was inspired by Stallone's enthusiastic speech on how to stay strong and never give up in the 2006 movie *Rocky Balboa* produced by MGM Studios. As Rocky Balboa, Stallone encounters his son on a street corner and provides him with inspirational words and advice. He mentions that life is hard and it can knock you down. But after you get hit, it is very important that you continue on. Stop pointing the finger at others; don't place the blame on them. Also, you can win in life if you believe in yourself.[2]

My late grandfather once gave me some words of wisdom about life and never giving up. He said, "In life you will face many hardships. There will be times when you will stumble and fall flat on your face. You will get bumps, bruises, scratches, a bloody nose, and a bloody lip. So what! Nothing ever comes easy, so get up and fight! Do not give up! Never give up! Keep moving ahead! If you give up, then it's over. A person must keep fighting on. Most importantly, keep the faith and you will succeed in life."

Yes! He truly meant what he said. We must keep going on in life and confront all our adversities. Most importantly, we must believe in ourselves and never give up no matter the obstacles in our way or the situation we face.

People must stop blaming others, society, and/or the government for their own problems or misfortunes. They must face them head-on.

Be strong and fight on! Never give up!

The other day, I met with an old friend, John, whom I have known since childhood. During our teenage years, we attended the Cub Scouts and Boy Scouts together and participated in baseball games. John was a great multisport athlete in high school and college. He also excelled academically and won numerous awards. He exhibited strong athletic skills and a competitive drive, never giving up.

John's tough mental attitude, his passion, and his drive to succeed in life made him a great athlete. He exhibited true grit when faced with adversity. This trait enabled him to face the biggest and most severe challenge he had ever faced in his life: a battle with cancer!

John confided in me and mentioned he recently had been diagnosed with colon cancer. He is undergoing chemotherapy and taking medications to fight the disease. He made no excuses for his sickness, not blaming God or anyone else for his dilemma. He faced the challenge as a true champion!

John relies on his positive outlook on life and his immense faith in God. He said, "I do not believe in defeat and surrender. I will not give up. I will fight this cancer head-on and until the end. God is by my side. With God's help, I will prevail. He has a plan for me. I place my total trust in God and no one else."

I consider John to be a living example of a person who is determined to live life and never give up. His powerful faith in God will help him succeed. Furthermore, John applies the principle of being strong and staying positive when faced with difficulties such as cancer. As a Christian, he is a fierce fighter and a faithful servant of God.

The Bible proclaims in 1 Corinthians 16:13, "Be on your guard, stay firm in the faith; be courageous; be strong!" (NIV).

Several years ago, I had the pleasure of meeting Melissa Farias, her husband Paul Espericueta, and several of their children during an adaptive sporting event for children and teenagers with disabilities. Their son Ashton, who is legally blind, participated in one leg of an adaptive triathlon consisting of swimming, biking, and walking/running. Ashton was noticeably excited about participating and was accompanied by a volunteer. After the event, Ashton and other participants joyfully received their individual medals. Ashton was extremely excited with a big smile while talking repeatedly to his family members and friends.

Later, I had the chance to coach Ashton in an adaptive basketball game under the auspices of Champions League Sports. I observed his tenacity, his unwillingness to give up, and his competitiveness with other participants. He did not allow his blindness to hinder his performance. I'd like to make special mention of his inner drive and motivation not to give up.

After the game, his mother smiled and said, "Ashton loves to compete, and he never gives up no matter what."

Days later I asked myself, *Where does this kid get the desire to compete in sporting events? What is his motivation? He is blind, but it doesn't faze him at all.*

Wow! I was inspired! I needed to interview him and find out the answers for myself.

I sought out his parents and decided to interview them at an appropriate time. Unfortunately, because I had to work and had personal matters to attend to, such as being hospitalized and battling cancer, I was unable to speak with his parents.

In May 2020, I spoke to Melissa over the phone and encouraged her to provide an account of her son Ashton, which she agreed to do. Melissa indicated she was previously married to Alfonso with two children and resided in Corpus Christi, Texas. She later became pregnant with her third child and visited an ob-gyn (obstetrician-gynecologist) during her twenty-sixth week of pregnancy, and the doctor provided some unsettling news. The examinations determined that her baby possibly had several medical problems, including spina bifida. Her primary doctor highly recommended she terminate the pregnancy. Melissa was startled and was provided with two nerve-wracking options: (1) follow doctor's orders and terminate her pregnancy or (2) make the decision herself and keep her baby. Melissa prayed fervently on the matter and chose the latter option: to keep her baby.

The doctors initially discovered the baby had spina bifida

and a small sac on the lower spine. They informed Melissa that a natural birth could be detrimental to the child, resulting in the rupture and tearing of the small sac, causing severe health issues or even death. Thus, Melissa underwent an emergency C-section during her thirty-eighth week of pregnancy.

In September 2008, her baby boy, named Ashton Pena, was born at Bay Area Hospital, Corpus Christi. He stayed at the hospital for ten days and later was transported to Driscoll Children's Hospital for further examination. There, he underwent a successful surgical procedure to repair the small, clear, paper-thin sac from his lower back.

Ashton was placed in the intensive care unit for two weeks and sadly developed hydrocephalus, causing fluid buildup in his brain cavity. He underwent a second major surgery, and a ventricular tube (shunt) was inserted in the back of his head to drain the excess fluid from his brain into his stomach.

I asked Melissa to describe Ashton's shunt, and she answered, "The shunt is a little pump that is surgically implanted in the right back side of his head with a tube that runs under his skin. It looks like a vein popping out. It then runs from the back of his head to the bottom of his neck and then into his stomach."

As per the medical professionals, Ashton would require the shunt for the rest of his life. If it were to be taken out, he would develop extra fluid in his head, which would drastically affect his vision, motor skills, and speech and would ultimately result in death.

After he was stabilized and had recovered from both surgeries, Ashton was discharged from the hospital. Melissa was provided with specific instructions on how to care for him. She was to lay Ashton down on his stomach and prevent him from turning onto his back because he'd just had back and head surgery. To lie in a different position would have been detrimental, negatively affecting the healing process. Melissa was extra careful and made it a priority to care properly for Ashton.

When Ashton reached three years of age, an unfortunate event occurred. Without anyone's knowledge, his shunt had become disconnected for an unspecified time.

Melissa commented, "After moving from one apartment to another one, we noticed that Ashton would get lost, would bump into the walls and furniture, and was unable to find his toys. Something was wrong with him. He was gradually losing his vision, and we did not know what the problem was."

During this time, Ashton spoke only three- or five-word sentences because the fluid from the disconnected shunt was having a detrimental effect on his speech. To help Ashton cope with others, a home health-care nurse provided him with occupational and physical therapy twice a week.

The family decided to relocate back to McAllen, Texas, and made sure Ashton was properly cared for.

Soon thereafter, Melissa took Ashton to a specialist eye doctor who conducted an eye examination for stigmatism. A week later Ashton was still running into things at home. Melissa took him back to the eye doctor for additional, in-depth eye examinations. The doctor concluded that Ashton was fine with no issues. Melissa voiced her concerns and told the doctor about Ashton's medical condition and the shunt implanted in the back of his head. The doctor requested she immediately contact Ashton's neurosurgeon in Corpus Christi for analysis. Melissa got in touch with the neurosurgeon, who instructed her to bring Ashton in immediately.

The following day, Melissa drove Ashton to Corpus Christi and met with the neurosurgeon. Ashton underwent a CT scan and an MRI, each displaying no visible problems. The neurosurgeon recommended exploratory surgery and requested the family's approval. The following day, Ashton underwent exploratory surgery, and the doctors unfortunately discovered a small leak in the shunt. The excessive fluid had built up and was putting a lot of pressure on his optic nerve. According to Melissa, Ashton had never complained about headaches, being tired, or anything else. He appeared normal.

The surgeons reconnected the shunt so the fluid could properly drain into the stomach. Ashton stayed in the hospital for one week. After his release, Melissa followed up with the eye specialist in Corpus Christi, following up again the next year.

Melissa declared, "As a mom, I was devastated! It was hard for me to adjust. And now I had to explain everything to Ashton. I was constantly guiding him by holding his hand and describing things to him such as colors and furniture. I never left him alone, for his own safety. This was new to me, and I did not know how to adjust or adapt to this situation."

I asked Melissa how she felt about Ashton's condition and if she ever questioned God. She replied, "Initially, I was upset. *Why? What did I do? What did he do to deserve this?* But I knew Ashton was my gift."

Melissa separated from her husband and eventually divorced him. Later she met a new boyfriend, Paul Espericueta, a sincere man who helped her with Ashton. Paul explained to her, "It is hard, but don't blame God. Things happen for a reason, and God does things for a reason. You cannot blame Him. God has a plan for everyone."

At the age of four, Ashton began learning braille, a system for blind people to communicate and read with raised dots. He utilized a Perkins braille machine, which resembles an old typewriter with six keys.

Ashton attended pre-K for two years, then kindergarten. He followed up with attendance at Roosevelt Elementary, located in south McAllen. Ashton loves attending school and is considered a super smart student with great grades.

He later transferred to Bonham Elementary in McAllen. At the time, he was the only blind student in school and was assigned an aide to shadow him all day long while at school.

Ashton used a cane or long walking stick to help him find his way around.

Ashton began participating in athletics by competing in his first ever blind tennis game. This adaptive sport utilizes a small foam ball filled with pellets and is inserted into a tennis ball to help blind people identify it by sound. Ashton enjoyed playing with others and requested to compete in other sports.

The family thereafter relocated to a two-story house and placed the furniture in its proper place before bringing Ashton inside. Paul was at Ashton's side most of the time helping him memorize the layout by counting the steps between pieces of furniture and to the different rooms. Ashton learned swiftly and had no trouble getting around the house or going from room to room.

Currently, Ashton is twelve years old and enrolled in the sixth grade at Cathey Middle School, McAllen, Texas. He competed in the spelling bee and won first place. Last year he was an active member of the junior varsity Chess Club. He really enjoyed playing chess and loved competing against other, regular kids. He has been involved in competitive chess for four years. He also participated in the Texas Chess Championship for elementary school students and placed ninth out of fifteen competitors. He subsequently qualified to compete in the United States National Chess Championship held in Nashville, Tennessee. But because of the coronavirus pandemic and safety concerns, the event was canceled. Ashton was extremely disappointed.

As a coach for Champions League Sports, I observed Ashton's competitiveness firsthand. It was particularly evident during his athletic performance in various adaptive sporting events such as basketball, baseball, soccer, and football. Ashton also participated twice as a swimmer in an adaptive triathlon relay race and won several medals. He always requested to wear a uniform in his favorite color, red. I made sure his special request was honored.

Ashton attends Mass at a Catholic church on Sundays with his parents and other family members. He also attends a Christian church with his biological dad, who sees him exclusively during weekend visitations.

Melissa commented, "I became aware that Ashton was not going to stop and let the disability hinder him from being a regular boy. His main motto in life is to never give up. I used to keep Ashton in a bubble. My husband would say, 'Ashton needs to get out and be a regular child. He needs to learn no matter if he is going to trip and fall.' This is the primary reason we involved Ashton in different sports."

She recalled one occasion when Ashton told her, "I will never give up because of my disability. I am not letting my disability stop me."

Several days ago, a teacher gave Ashton an assignment and asked him why he liked chess and what he got out of it. Ashton replied, "I am not going to let my disability stop me from doing the things I like."

Melissa was in awe She said, "Wow! The word *can't* is not in Ashton's vocabulary. I tell Ashton and my other kids, 'You can't say "I can't" unless you try.'"

I was able to speak to Ashton, who commented in a soft voice, "I love chess because it is incredibly challenging and helps me improve my critical thinking skills." I asked Ashton if he likes the competitive aspect, and he replied, "Yes!" Then he said, "I don't let my disability stop me from doing anything." His recommendation to other kids with a disability is, "Keep moving forward. Don't let anything stop you."

Melissa provided a final recommendation to families who have a child with a disability: "Let your child be a normal child. Also, pray and don't lose faith."

We must not quit when faced with adversity. No matter what challenges or difficulties we face, we must confront them head-on and continue fighting. Life will always be a struggle. I recommend that you not give up and instead seek the assistance of a family member, a friend, or an associate, and most importantly God.

A brave person mentioned in the Bible is David the shepherd boy. He was faced with overwhelming odds when battling against the giant Goliath. David demonstrated bravery, courage, and a "never give up" attitude when facing the mighty foe Goliath, known as the champion of the Philistines. David had tremendous faith in God and was extremely upset with Goliath's comments as noted in 1 Samuel 17:36–37, where David declares, "Seeing he [Goliath] hath defied the armies of the living God … [the Lord] … will deliver me out of the hand of this Philistine."

David prevailed with a sling and a smooth stone, which he slung and which struck Goliath on the forehead, killing him instantly. David's story is one of a young man who has total trust in the Lord to protect him against his adversary. David did not give into fear or doubt and was able to accomplish the impossible. As noted in Luke 11:39, "For with God nothing shall be impossible." The impossible had occurred again as David received a special calling from God as noted in the Bible. First Samuel 16:13 says, "The Spirit of the Lord came upon David from that day forward." He later became King David and ruled Israel. There are many other stories in the Bible about other individuals who exhibited strong faith, courage, and trust in God.

Our journey through life will never be easy. Life will never be easy! Each of us will face many obstacles and struggles. At times we will doubt God's love for us. But we must endure the hardships and the pain and put our best foot forward. God loves us all. Let us put our trust and faith in Him!

I leave you with this final thought: Don't give up. Continue your wonderful journey through life graciously provided to you by Almighty God.

I pray that God blesses you. Trust in God! Believe in Him!

CHAPTER 8

---꙳ ✄ ꙳---

CONCLUSION

God only knowns what lies ahead for us in our lives, the challenges and struggles we will have to face to succeed in life and draw closer to Him. God desires only the best for us. He loves us and formed us in His own image.

We must trust in God and hold onto our faith! We must keep going in life, taking one step at a time, not being selfish but helping others in need along the way, especially the less fortunate and those with disabilities.

Do not let an empty void fill your heart. Instead, fill it with love. Share your love with others. Embrace God's love for everyone, a beautiful love filled with peace and joy.

When your mind begins to wander off and you feel like giving up, thinking you have been defeated by whatever adversary you are facing, do not give up. Giving up is not the solution. Stay strong and keep fighting! Continue the good fight!

Most importantly, trust in God and in our Lord and Savior Jesus Christ. Many blessings to you!

I will say of the Lord, "He is my refuge and my fortress: my God, in him will I trust."

—Psalm 91:2

NOTES

Chapter 1: Trust in God

[1] George Washington, "Thanksgiving Proclamation, 3 October 1789," National Archives—Founders Online, https://founders.archives.gov/ documents/Washington/05-04-02-0091, accessed May 22, 2024.

Chapter 2: Keeping the Faith

[1] ACS Medical Content and News Staff, "Facts & Figures: 2021 Reports Another Record-Breaking 1-Year Drop in Cancer Deaths," January 12, 2021, American Cancer Society, www.cancer.org/research/acs-research-news/facts-and-figures-2021.html, accessed August 28, 2022.

Chapter 4: God's Children

[1] "Law for the Prevention of Progeny with Hereditary Diseases," 2015, Weebly, https://www.deadlymedicine.weebly.com/law-for-the-prevention-of-progeny-with-hereditary-diseasesrdquo.html.

[2] Ibid.

[3] "Dear Church, Children with Special Needs Are God's Children Too," October 8, 2018, Raising the Extraordinary, https:// raisingtheextraordinary.com /church-special-needs/, accessed August 30, 2022.

[4] Ibid.

[5] Tony Attwood, *The Complete Guide to Asperger's Syndrome* (London and Philadelphia: Jessica Kingsley, 2007), 7.

Chapter 5: Expect Miracles

[1] Dictionary.com, s.v. "miracle," accessed May 22, 2024, https://www. dictionary.com/browse/miracle.

Chapter 6: Keep Praying

[1] "The Power of Prayer: Theological Foundations," May 8, 2020, Grace College,. https://online.grace.edu/news/the-power-of-prayer-theological-foundations-at-grace-college-online/.

[2] Andrea Monda, "The Conversion Story of C. S. Lewis," EWTN, https://www.ewtn.com/catholicism/library/conversion-story-of-c-s-lewis-9821.

Chapter 7: Never Give Up

[1] Tori Couch, "Martina Navratilova Announced as Executive Women's Day Luncheon Speaker," April 12, 2024, *360West*, https://360westmagazine.com/features/2024/04/martina-navratilova-announced-as-executive-womens-day-luncheon-speaker/.

[2] *Rocky Balboa*, directed by Sylvester Stallone (Culver City: MGM Studios, 2006).

PHOTOGRAPHS

Chapter 1: Trust in God

1 The author, Aurelio Leal, and his spouse,
Esmeralda Leal, out on date night.

*2 The author with his two sons, Aurelio Matthew
Leal and Daniel A. Leal, on a hunting trip.*

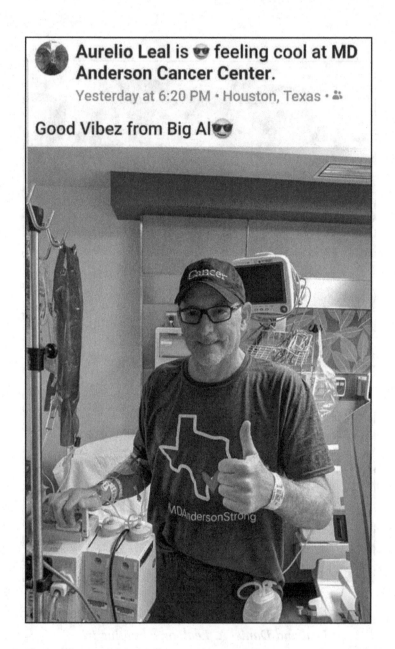

3 The author at MD Anderson Hospital, Houston, Texas, 2019.

4 The author at MD Anderson Hospital, Houston, Texas, 2019.

Chapter 2: Keeping the Faith

5 Leopolda Martinez, birthday celebration.

6 Leopolda Martinez playing a slot machine.

*7 Stephanie Wilson with her son Jason Wilson
enjoying the beach at South Padre Island, Texas.*

8 *Jason Wilson, graduation.*

Chapter 3: Unconditional Love

9 Mary Jane Lopez and her daughter Viva Selena Marie Lopez.

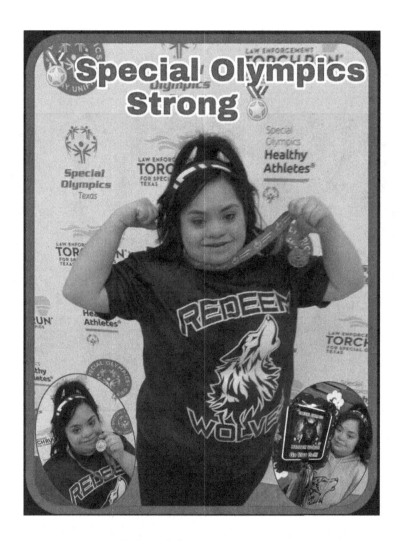

10 Viva Selena Marie Lopez.

11 The author with Art "Good Times"
Benavides at a hunting ranch.

12 Art "Good Times" Benavides at a fishing pond.

Chapter 4: God's Children

13 Maritza Ramirez.

14 Maritza Ramirez.

Chapter 5: Expect Miracles

15 Sammy Gomez celebrating World Down Syndrome Day.

16 Sammy Gomez at the awards podium receiving a medal after an adaptive sporting event.

Chapter 6: Keep Praying

17 Mary Cruz Costilla and her son Danny Costilla.

*18 Danny Costilla, a medal winner, at
an adaptive sporting event.*

19 Nena Almaguer and her son, Miguel Almaguer, at a celebration event.

20 Miguel Almaguer dressed as a cowboy.

Chapter 7: Never Give Up

21 Lorenzo Tijerina proudly carrying the US flag.

22 *Lorenzo Tijerina posing with a Dallas Cowboys cheerleader.*

23 Ashton Espericueta at the Texas Big Game Awards.

24 Ashton Espericueta, medal winner at the
2022 University Interscholastic League.

ACKNOWLEDGMENTS

To my late parents, Aurelio Leal Sr. and Juanita Leal Rodriguez, whom I dearly love and miss. You provided all the inspiration and support I needed in my life.

Esmeralda Leal, my wife, I am extremely grateful for your unwavering love.

A special thanks to the following individuals whose stories, which they shared with me, are a great addition to *Trusting in God's Plan*: Leopolda Martinez (a.k.a. Pola); Stephanie Wilson and Jason Wilson; Mary Jane Lopez and Viva Lopez; Mr. Art "Good Times" Benavidez and Josie Benavidez; Daniel A. Leal; Maritza Esqueda (founder of the Greater Gold Foundation); Ira Cobos and Chauncy Cobos; Hilario, Ileana, and Samuel "Sammy" Gomez; Maricruz Costilla and Danny Costilla; Nena Almaguer and Miguel Almaguer; Lorenzo Tijerina; and Melissa Farias and Ashton Farias.

A sincere thanks to the late Eduardo "Eddie" Vela and his wife, Brandy Vela, founders of Faith, Family, & Friends Foundation.

Aunt Hilda Trevino: thanks for your encouragement, for your moral support, and for your editorial review of my book. I will forever be grateful.

A profound thanks to the following nonprofit organizations, which have raised awareness and provided support to the special needs community in the Rio Grande Valley of South Texas: Disability Chamber of Commerce–RGV, Capable Kids Foundation (Champions League Sports), Bebo's Angels, Team Mario, Big Heroes Inc., and the Down Syndrome Association of South Texas.

My friend John: Never give up. Continue with your faith and trust in God.

To all the members of iUniverse: Your outstanding teamwork led to the successful publication of *Trusting in God's Plan*.

To all my readers: Thanks for your purchase. May God Bless you.

ABOUT THE AUTHOR

Aurelio (Al) Leal is a retired FBI special agent who served more than thirty years with the United States government. He is a Christian, devoted husband, and father. He has been married to Esmeralda Casanova Leal for twenty-four years and has two loving sons, Aurelio Matthew Leal and Daniel Alejandro Leal. Mr. Leal resides in Edinburg, Texas, which is in the Rio Grande Valley of South Texas, where he spends his time as a private investigator, security consultant, and author.

Mr. Leal was diagnosed with appendiceal cancer (adenocarcinoma of the appendix), also known pseudomyxoma peritonea, in January 2019. He underwent two intense, life-threatening surgeries, one in San Antonio, Texas, and one at MD Anderson Hospital in Houston. Mr. Leal miraculously recovered and was recently given a clean bill of health by his doctors, having been declared cancer-free. He still travels every six months to MD Anderson Hospital for biyearly checkups. Having had this deadly disease has compelled him to value life more and has intensified his faith and trust in God.

Besides exercising, Mr. Leal loves the outdoors and spends his time fishing, hunting, and golfing, also vacationing with his family. He is a strong advocate for children and adults with several types of disabilities, people who are battling cancer, and United States veterans who have made the ultimate sacrifice, giving their time and their lives so that we may live free.

Printed in the United States
by Baker & Taylor Publisher Services